Office
Finances
Made Easy

Office
Finances
Made Easy

A Get-Started Guide to Budgets, Purchasing, and Financial Statements

Robert G. Finney

AMACOM
American Management Association
New York • Atlanta • Boston • Chicago • Kansas City • San Francisco • Washington, D.C.
Brussels • Mexico City • Tokyo • Toronto

Special discounts on bulk quantities of AMACOM books are available to corporations, professional associations, and other organizations. For details, contact Special Sales Department, AMACOM, an imprint of AMA Publications, a division of American Management Association,
1601 Broadway, New York, NY 10019.
Tel.: 212-903-8316   Fax: 212-903-8083

This publication is designed to provide accurate and authoritative information in regard to the subject matter covered. It is sold with the understanding that the publisher is not engaged in rendering legal, accounting, or other professional service. If legal advice or other expert assistance is required, the services of a competent professional person should be sought.

Library of Congress Cataloging-in-Publication Data

Finney, Robert G.
    Office finances made easy : a get-started guide to budgets, purchasing, and financial statements / Robert G. Finney,
        p.   cm.
    Includes index.
    ISBN 0-8144-7061-0
    1. Business enterprises—Finance.   2. Budget in business.
3. Purchasing.   4. Financial statements.   I. Title.
HG4026.F5273   2000
658.15—dc21   99-33974
                                                          CIP

Printing number

10 9 8 7 6 5 4 3 2 1

Table of Contents

Office
Finances
Made Easy

Introduction

The lifeblood of business is people who can do the things that business operations need, ranging from designing and selling to organizing and administering. However, every business must make money to continue to exist. Therefore, the most valuable employees, and the most promotable, are those who are proficient in money matters as well as operating talents.

Office Finances Made Easy: A Get-Started Guide to Budgets, Purchasing, and Financial Statements is a practical book designed to help you understand and successfully apply the three financial disciplines that office professionals continually encounter in their work: budgeting, purchasing, and financial statement analysis. A Glossary of Financial Terms concludes the book.

Office professionals get involved in budgeting in a variety of ways. All may have to supply information about their own work, some may have to help their bosses prepare their budgets, some may be responsible for their office's budgets, and some may even have to coordinate a number of organizational unit budgets. Part I, "Powerful Budgeting," explains the nature and work of budgeting and covers handling uncertainty, defining and planning the work, generating the budget numbers, and getting the budget approved.

Similarly, office professionals specify and use purchases or actually buy them. In either case, they have a role in making the company's purchasing effective and efficient. In addition to knowing how buying is done, understanding purchasing's place in the business will help them carry out that role. Part II, "Effective Purchasing," provides an understanding of purchasing by defining the requirements and trade-offs and the techniques and practices that satisfy all of the various requirements.

Part III, "Fruitful Financial Statement Analysis," narrows this major subject to the direct working concern of office professionals: not investments, but whether their own companies, competitors, and vendors will *survive* in a healthy and successful condition. It covers defining and understanding problems if they exist. Part III also provides an explanation and analysis of the cash flow statements, balance sheets, and profit and loss statements, plus associated information and multistatement analysis.

Mastering these three elements of office money can quickly improve the personal money—salaries— of office professionals.

Part I

Powerful Budgeting

1

The Nature of Budgeting

The budget is the financial plan of a company for a period of one year. All sizable businesses prepare budgets, all managers and their key people (who we will call the "budgeters") are involved in them, and all employees are affected by them.

Why annual budgets? Investors and lenders evaluate companies based on annual periods (and, to a lesser extent, quarters of a year). Because the budget is both a plan and a scorecard, it must focus on those same annual and quarterly time periods.

Our subject is the work of budgeting from the point of view of the budgeters. We need not be concerned (except to provide context) with budgeting theories or what the president or the controller will do with the budget; nor do we need to become experts in accounting or investment analysis.

What budgeters need from budgeting is definition of required work and outputs next year, approval of the resources needed to accomplish that work and those outputs, and the inputs and support that they will receive from other elements of the company.

Office professionals get involved in budgeting in a variety of ways. All may have to supply information about their own work. Secretaries and administrative assistants may have to help their bosses prepare their organizations' budgets. Office managers are probably responsible for their office budgets and may coordinate other unit budgets in smaller companies. Accordingly, the budgeting content in this book is not limited to information about budget inputs; it is designed to provide general understanding of budgets and the budgeting process.

The Importance of Budgeting

The budget is, first of all, a forecast of the year's financial results, for the company as a whole and for all its organizational elements. Beyond this, it is three other important things: a plan of the year's work, a communication of management's real objectives and priorities, and a principal control and measurement tool.

The budget is the *only* instrument that can give reality to objectives, strategies, priorities, and plans. Whatever management wants to accomplish cannot be done unless resources have been provided for that accomplishment. Similarly, goals take on meaning when reflected in the budget and have no meaning otherwise. Marketing may rave about a new product idea, but you know that management does not consider it important if there are no funds in the budget for its design. Conversely, a large design budget for that product shows that its management priority is indeed high.

The budget is used to control budgeters' activities, and their performance is measured against those budgets. All elements of the company have to explain deviations and probably cannot get new activities approved unless they are budgeted. Good things happen to people who meet or beat their budgets, while those who miss their budgets lose favor, or worse.

From the viewpoint of office professionals, budgets enable them to get the "tools" and help they need to do their jobs. If you need a junior associate or a new computer to get your work done, of course you have to convince your boss of the need and the payoff. However, if funds for those tools and help are not in the budget, chances are that your boss will not be able to authorize them, even if convinced of their need.

If you are responsible for a budget, keep in mind that a good budget explains what your organization can and cannot do; explains the support you need to meet your commitments; sets realistic goals for you and your people; helps you communicate with bosses, subordinates, and other organizations; and shows your understanding of the company's financial realities. Therefore, it helps you improve your operations and shows that you are ready for promotion.

If you are not responsible for a budget, then you and your work are part of your boss's budget. If you can influence your boss to budget your work and needs properly, you have a leg up on doing a good job next year. However, a poor budget—one that does not correctly reflect your needs and what you can accomplish—will handicap you all year.

Why Budgeting Is So Difficult

Because budgeting is so important, it is unfortunate that it is also difficult, and you need to understand why. It is not because of bad people; the best and the brightest have difficulty with budgeting.

Budgets can never be perfect because they deal with the always uncertain future. Pessimists promise poorer results than they believe are achievable, as a hedge against this uncertainty. Optimists assume that only good things will happen. In either case, the budget is less probable than all its specific numbers imply. If the uncertainty is not treated deliberately, it will later be difficult to determine whether good or bad results came from performance or luck.

In addition to this future uncertainty, budgets can never be easy for three main reasons. First, top management wants a budget that plans the best results possible. Individual budgeters want to work for a profitable, healthy company, but they primarily want budgets that they can beat. They are measured on their performance versus budget and want to make sure they don't promise too much.

Second, every company has important outside factors that it cannot control: market health, competitors' actions, new laws, tight credit, and so on. Also, all budgeters have internal uncontrollable factors: things decided in other parts of the company, such as product availability for a sales budgeter. The only thing certain about these uncontrollable factors is that some of them will change surprisingly.

Third, budgeting always has been, and always will be, a psychological process. Because of the uncertainty and other difficulties, both boss and subordinate must attempt to estimate the other's state of mind. Each maneuvers to get the budget to their "best" numbers: best results possible for the boss, numbers that can be beaten for the subordinate. There is nothing sinister in this; if the people are good, the final compromise will probably be good. The problem is that the psychology sometimes overwhelms reality and causes long sessions, time pressure, and emotion on both sides.

In short, budgets are difficult because they deal with next year, about which many things are uncertain and uncontrollable. For the part that can be known, the people who know best, the budgeters directly involved, are not motivated to accept the most challenging budgets. The finished budget is then treated as gospel and used to measure the budgeters.

These inherent problems will never go away; they must be dealt with and neutralized by competent budgeting.

The Budgeting Process

Preparation of the budget usually begins three to four months before the budget year begins. Thus, for a company whose fiscal year is the calendar year, budgeting probably starts in September.

We will discuss the company budgeting process in five parts:

1. Budget forms and instructions are distributed to all budgeters.
2. Budget forms are filled out and submitted.
3. Individual budgets are transformed into appropriate budgeting/accounting terms.
4. Individual budgets are consolidated into one overall company budget.
5. The budget is reviewed, modified as necessary, and approved.

Budget Forms

No two companies' budget forms are exactly alike. You must learn your own company's forms from your boss or accounting. We will not discuss variations in forms here, but only the kind of information required plus a simple example.

Most company budgets take the same form as the financial statements—profit and loss (P&L), balance sheet, and cash flow—that appear in the annual report, with two additions:

- There is more detail and elaboration in particular areas where the president wants more visibility: revenue by product line, for example.
- Budgets include quarterly and often monthly numbers, rather than just year-end predictions. Management needs to track results frequently, so timely action can be taken if needed.

The company budget thus probably predicts revenue, expense, profit, capital expenditure, and cash flow expected each month during the year; and the value of balance sheet accounts like inventory, equipment, accounts payable, and long-term debt at the end of each month.

The lowest unit budget, the first building block of that company budget, typically requires three types of information:

- Costs
- Outputs
- Supplemental information

By far the most information required is predicted *costs*. The budgeter may be asked for "effort" descriptions—man-hours of effort, numbers of items purchased, etc.—that the accountants convert into dollars, or the budgeter may be asked to supply dollar numbers. Depending on the unit's function, cost prediction may be required in considerable detail.

An engineering unit, for example, is usually required to forecast costs by project because management wants to track each project.

Whether the predicted *outputs* of the unit are required depends on its function. Examples of functions for which outputs are required in the budget are numbers of different items completed by an assembly unit and numbers of orders of different products by a sales unit. Such outputs are "financially significant," meaning that they ultimately relate directly to revenue. On the other hand, the number of pages expected to be produced by a word processing unit—its primary output—has no direct relationship to revenue, so its predicted outputs are probably not required on the budget form.

Required *supplemental information* varies widely, but includes information that helps explain the budget (e.g., the number of cold calls per period planned by a sales function as a basis for the orders prediction), helps evaluate the budget (e.g., results for the previous three years for comparison), and the like. The assumptions made in preparing the budget are also often required as supplemental information.

As an example of a budget form, the following payroll budget form is about as simple as budget forms get.

Payroll Budget Form

Year: 20xx	J	F	M	A	M	J	J	A	S	O	N	D	TOTAL
Salaries ($000)													
(Name)													
(Name)													
(Name)													
New hire													
Total													
Benefits ($000)													
Other Indirect Costs ($000)													
Travel & living													
Telephone expense													
Subscriptions													
Training													
Outside services													
Other													
Total													
Total cost													

Supplemental Information
  Assumptions:
  New hires (number and date):
  Central computer hours (per month):

Total cost is the sum of total salaries, fringe benefits (medical insurance and the like), and total other indirect costs (as itemized). Labor costs are just salaries, readily identified and tracked by individual names. The number and type of "other indirect" cost lines is determined by management's decision concerning the desired visibility of different kinds of costs. Every budget has an "other" category for costs not itemized, because the budget must include total costs. Typically, outputs are not required in a payroll unit budget.

Most budget forms require more information than this simple example and may run for pages and pages. Take as an example a factory assembly function. The assembly manager is asked for number of assemblies by item (i.e., its outputs), direct labor man-hours by project or product, indirect labor, and more varieties of other indirect costs, all by month. Supplemental information probably includes such things as predicted direct and indirect head count, machine usage in hours, new hires, and layoffs. All of these items have to be predicted for each month of the year or at least for each quarter.

Instructions for completing the budget usually accompany the forms, or are transmitted at about the same time. They contain the detailed schedule for the whole company budgeting process, culminating with presentation to the board of directors. They also should include the assumptions and ground rules to be used throughout the company, division, or department. General guidance, goals, and priorities for budget preparation are usually given. Procedures and budget are included, and any changes from the previous year are usually noted and explained.

Completion and Submission of Budget Forms

This is the budgeter's activity of actually preparing the budget, the subject of the rest of this book. Because it is so central to our purpose, the work of budgeting is covered separately in chapter 2.

Transformation

The transformation of budgets is done by accounting. If budgeters submit budget numbers in terms of items and man-hours, these are translated into dollars. Allocated costs are added into the unit budgets. Burden rates are computed and applied when and as appropriate.

Any *activity* formats used at lower organizational levels (man-hours, purchased items, transactions, etc.) are transformed ultimately into the *financial* format (revenue, expense, cash flow, and balance sheet items) used for the overall company budget. The budgets used by higher management are in a format that presents the information desired to manage the business, typically a mixture of financial and activity formats.

What are "allocated costs" and "burden rates?" Before proceeding, it is appropriate to pause and define these important accounting concepts for budgeters:

Allocated Costs, Cost Burdens, and Burden Rates

Allocated costs are costs of one type that are assigned or charged to costs of other types. Every company has costs that are incurred and paid separately from its organizational units but that are either used by the units (such as facility and telephone costs) or are general costs of doing business (such as management, legal, and accounting costs). Many such costs are typically charged, or allocated, to each unit of the particular business, based on mathematical formulas. For example, facility costs may be charged to a particular unit based on the square feet of space it occupies times the cost of the facility (rent, utilities, taxes) per square foot.

Cost burdens are the amount of costs added to a particular cost as the result of allocating another type of cost to it. Managements universally want to know the profitability of individual products that they sell. For a manufacturing business, for example, they define direct costs as labor, materials, and other things that are directly related to producing the product. However, there are many costs that are necessary but only indirectly related to a particular product, everything from the manufacturing manager's salary to the costs of the human resources function. All such things are called *indirect costs*. Traditionally, direct costs are "burdened" with certain indirect costs to get a better measure of product profitability; that is, such indirect costs are a "cost burden" on the direct costs.

Burden rates are the rates at which these cost burdens are applied. If total indirect labor costs in the example manufacturing business are expected to be twice the total direct labor costs for the year, this defines a burden rate called *manufacturing labor overhead rate*, equal to 200 percent. In this case, every dollar of direct labor involved in making a product results in three dollars being charged to that particular product. That is, $1 + ($1 \times 200$ percent $) = 3.

Different businesses use various burdens and burden rates. Common ones are manufacturing labor overhead rate, manufacturing material overhead rate, engineering overhead rate, and general and administrative (G&A) rate. The latter is used to allocate G&A expense, which is a necessary expense that cannot even be indirectly related to the production of products or services, such as the costs of the

president's office, board of directors, accounting, and human resources. G&A is often allocated to entire product or service lines based
on their sales or cost of sales.

Consolidation

The company budget is really a collection of budgets that predict its important financial results: orders, sales, P&L, capital expenditures, cash
flow, and balance sheet.

All organizational units contribute costs to the company budget,
some forecast orders and revenue or sales, and some budget capital expenditures. *Capital expenditures* are costs for equipment, facilities,
and the like, that are expected to be used for a number of years. They
are budgeted and accounted for (as "fixed assets") separately from most
costs, which are charged to the P&L, or "expensed." Balance sheet and
cash flow budgets are ordinarily done by accounting and usually do not
involve budgeters beyond their cost and revenue inputs.

The company budget is built as a consolidation of budgets that match
its organization structure. For example, consider the structure of a
midsize product company with a functional organization reporting to
the president:

    Company
            Marketing
            Sales
            Engineering
            Manufacturing
            Finance
            Human resources

Each of these major departments, of course, has an organizational
structure within it; for simplicity, let's detail only the sales department
(assuming only domestic sales and a geographical sales organization):

    Sales
            Eastern region sales
                    New England branch
                    Mid-Atlantic branch
                    Southeastern branch

Central region sales
   Northern branch
   Southern branch
   Midwestern branch
Western region sales
   Southwestern branch
   Northwestern branch
   Rocky Mountain branch
Sales administration

Within the sales department, the first budgets generated are those for each of the branches. All the Eastern region branch budgets are then consolidated into the Eastern region budget. The budgets of the three regions plus sales administration are then consolidated into the sales department budget. At the same time, the budgets of the other departments are built, level by level, in the same way. Finally, the company budget is the consolidation of all the department budgets.

The budget at each level is the summation of all the budgets at the next lower level, plus the costs and other budget items associated with the manager at that level. There is also summarization of information at each level upward and transformation from activity to financial formats.

Review, Modification, and Approval

Transformation and consolidation are interleaved with this final step. Together, they are a step-by-step, repetitive progression up the levels of the organization.

The first review is by the budgeter's boss. All the unit budgets for the boss's organization will have been consolidated to give the boss a first look at the overall budget. In this review, the budgeter is expected to explain, justify, and defend the submitted numbers. With the help of accounting, there are comparisons with the budgets of interacting organizations to check consistency.

When the boss has approved all subordinate budgets, the process is repeated at the next level. The boss's budget is transformed and consolidated with peer organizations to provide the budget for the manager at the next higher level. That manager then reviews the budgets of all his or her subordinates, and so on.

Each review may cause changes, which then have to be reflected back down the organization. This process can take months and be full of surprises for all budgeters. They might believe, more than once, that their budgets have been approved, only to find expenses cut and/or outputs increased *again* as a result of review by higher management.

This iterative process ends with final review (which might result in yet another round of changes) and approval of the total company budget by the board of directors. This board review is typically held at the last board meeting before the new budget year begins. After board approval, the final budgets are distributed to all managers.

2

The Work of Budgeting Amidst Uncertainty

As noted in chapter 1, all budgeters are required to predict their units' costs for next year. Some have to forecast the outputs that can be achieved: revenue, shipments, assemblies, transactions, service repair calls, and the like. Many budgeters also have to supply supplemental forecasts of various kinds.

Now, no organizational unit exists in a vacuum, self-contained in its work. All units need inputs and support *from* other organizational elements, and all units supply outputs *to* other elements that those functions need as inputs and support for their work. In a factory, the shipping function is the only one that has outputs direct to the customer; all other factory units hand their outputs to other internal organizations. Thus, another important result of budgeting is each unit's definition of its needs from, and outputs to, other organizational elements within the company. This is required to ensure that the whole company is going in the same direction to carry out the desired strategy.

Thus, budgeters are required to generate good predictions for next year of the following:

- Expected costs
- Achievable outputs
- Requested supplemental information
- Needs from and outputs to other organizational elements within the company

The Work

The budgeter's work in meeting these requirements consists of two related tasks: planning next year's work and generating the numbers.

15

Planning Next Year's Work

To supply these required budgeting outputs or results, budgeters and their key people must first answer a set of questions:

- What are we expected to accomplish?
- How are we going to accomplish it? (That is, what processes and activities are going to be involved in getting our work done?)
- What inputs and support do we need, and can we get, from other organizations within and outside the company?
- What kinds of effort, purchases, services, and costs are involved in getting our work done?
- How do we know everything we are being told now won't change as the year moves along?

What have we just said? *Budgeters must first plan their work for next year.* This is the first component of the work of budgeting.

A plan tells how you are going to get from point A to point B. In business plans in general, point A is the set of resources, skills, processes, and working environment that your unit now possesses, and point B is the set of things that need to be accomplished. For the budget, point B is the set of things to be accomplished *next year.*

Planning the work requires that the unit's work must first be understood, so a prerequisite is *defining the work.* This takes effort, but it is effort that managers should expend anyway, just to do their jobs.

Once the work is defined and understood, the outputs expected of the unit over the next year, with the required schedule, must be identified. Similarly, the kinds and amounts of input and support that will be available, and when, must be determined. Then, how you are going to do the work must be decided. This is all discussed in chapter 3.

The wild card in this work planning is the inherent uncertainty of the future, reflected in the last question in the set of questions at the beginning of this section of the chapter. However, the uncertainty makes the planning more important, not less. (If you *knew* what would happen, you wouldn't have to plan, would you?) The uncertainty cannot be avoided—future uncertainty is not resolved until time passage makes the future the present—but it can be handled and its effects minimized. Future uncertainty looms so large in budgeting that handling it is discussed in this chapter, before work planning and number generation.

Generating the Numbers

All the planning work counts for nothing if you predict the output and cost numbers poorly. For example, you can be perfect in thinking through every single step involved in painting a house; however, if your estimates of the amount of paint needed and the time required are way off, your cost estimate will be worthless.

Generating the budget numbers properly is the second component of the work of budgeting. In reality, of course, the work of generating these numbers is not divorced from the planning work of budgeting. Indeed, predicting the numbers is the result, and the natural last step, of the planning. However, it is appropriate to discuss number generation separately, because there is a right way and a number of wrong ways to choose the numbers that actually go into the budget. In the house-painting example, the right way to estimate labor would be to plan all the steps—cleaning, spackling, walls, trim, etc.—and estimate each from experience. A wrong way could be to base labor hours on total square feet without regard for the particular preparation required.

Information on how to generate the budget numbers is presented in chapter 4.

Handling Uncertainty

The biggest difficulty in developing budgets is the fact that the future is always uncertain. You can't get rid of this uncertainty by doing more work or crunching more numbers. Nor will spending an extra month on the budget really help. That will only reduce the time element of uncertainty by a month out of a prediction time of more than twelve months. As for starting the budget later, that will only make your preparation more frantic, because it still has to be finished before the budget year begins, a minimum prediction time of twelve months.

This uncertainty permeates all aspects of budgeting, so it makes sense to discuss how to handle it before proceeding to the rest of our subjects.

Kinds of Uncertainty in Budgeting

The simplest kind of uncertainty is temporary uncertainty, meaning information known by someone in the company but not communicated to you in time for budget submission. Typical examples are the number of each product that will have to be produced, what responsibilities your unit will have toward a new remote location, and the specific territory to be covered by a sales branch. This kind of uncertainty is really only lack of communication. The solution for it is simply to dig out the information, seeking whatever help you need to find it.

Then there is normal planning uncertainty; for example, you are probably not certain of your labor costs for a particular project you have to forecast for next year. This kind of uncertainty is tackled by knowledge, capability, and experience. Managers and their key people get paid partly to plan things well, and chapter 3 will help them achieve that goal.

The type of uncertainty that makes budgeting so difficult can be called *inherent uncertainty*. That is, no matter how smart and experienced you are, you cannot predict such things as interest rates, particular customer decisions, commodity prices, and the like. (If the experts are often wrong in predicting interest rates, how can we expect to predict them correctly?)

There are two kinds of inherent uncertainty for a budgeter. First, every company has external factors that have important effects on their results—various industry, market, economic, government, and financial factors.

Second, all budgeters also face internal company factors that strongly affect their costs and outputs. These are things dictated in other parts of the company and beyond their own control. Examples are purchasing and personnel policies, employee benefit levels, production schedules, marketing priorities, and the like.

The distinction between external and internal factors is real, but both are handled the same way. The key to each is that they are *uncontrollable* by the budgeters that they affect. A purchasing unit's workload is affected by the economy, for example, boom times make prompt material delivery more difficult, and by the company's production needs. Neither of these factors can be influenced by the purchasing manager.

The inherent uncertainties are our prime concerns; temporary and planning uncertainties can be resolved by good work, while the inherent uncertainties won't go away until the future becomes the present.

Explicit Assumptions

How is this inherent uncertainty ordinarily handled? You can get advice from bosses, experts, and your favorite media prophet, and knowledge and experience help. But let's face it—the only thing you can do about an inherent uncertainty is to guess. (The bosses, experts, and the media prophet are guessing, too.) That is, you *make an assumption* about what will happen or about the cost, price, or value of an important item in next year's budget.

The problem is that most budgeters make *implicit* assumptions. That is, they are never identified as assumptions but just carried along with the cost and other numbers that are developed. Then, midway through the year, if the budget is being missed, no one remembers any assumptions; they just focus on the fact that the budget is being missed.

The right way to do it is to make *explicit* assumptions. The guesses made about important uncertainties are prominently noted when made. They are then carried along with the budget numbers (as supplementary information with the budget forms) throughout the review and approval process. All the budget planning and numbers are made consistent with the assumptions, and are changed if the assumptions change.

An Illustration

As a company-level example, consider an American company that has a substantial Japanese subsidiary and does a large amount of business there. Accounting rules require that the balance sheet in Japanese yen be revalued in American dollars on the American parent company's balance sheet.

Because of this conversion into dollars, a fall or rise in the value of the yen against the dollar generates profits or losses completely outside the control of the company. Thus, it is appropriate to handle the yen–dollar relationship with an explicit budgetary assumption about the average rate for the year in question. The budgeted currency profit or loss is then simply based on this assumption. If at any time during the year there is a large move in the yen versus the dollar, it will be understood that the cause of profit variance from budget is not a reflection of the performance of the business.

What happens without an explicit assumption? Currency profit or loss is then just part of the profit budget that the subsidiary is expected to meet. If the yen–dollar rate changes greatly during the year (which is probable), subsidiary management either gets a windfall or has a problem not of its own making. If the latter, there will be pressure to cut some planned, productive activity to get back on budget. A good strategy may be crippled by cost cuts brought on totally by an uncontrollable event that has no bearing on how well the company is performing.

Benefits of Explicit Assumptions

The emotional climate of budgeting mostly arises out of the uncertainty of the future. Explicit assumptions are an antidote for emotion. They do away with statements by your boss like, "You won't need five more people because next year's economy is going to be poor." You and your boss can first rationally discuss your assumptions and simply change them to your boss's preference if there is disagreement. Then the two of you can focus on your costs and outputs—the proper subject for budget discussions—under the assumed conditions. You can avoid the psychological games of (You) "I have to pad my budget to handle all the uncertainty," and (Boss) "I have to find where he or she is sandbagging the budget." Instead, the discussion becomes (Both) "Given the assumed conditions, how can we maximize unit output and minimize unit cost?"

There are other benefits. All management is made to realize better how decisions made in one part of the company will affect other parts. Distinguishing the "external uncontrollables" allows management to understand and focus on the controllable factors—the things that it can influence and change. Explicit assumptions also allow fairer measurement, as is clear in the Japanese subsidiary illustration. Finally, morale and performance are improved; most people accept challenges if convinced that the boss understands the problems and will measure them fairly.

Making Useful Budgeting Assumptions

Making proper budgeting assumptions is not a trivial task. If you start with a general assumption like, "Inflation will be 3 percent next year," you still have to reason through how such an inflation rate will affect your unit's costs.

At the other extreme, your bosses will not let you get away with an assumption like, "We will reduce our costs 15 percent next year." Such a statement baldly assumes that you will do your job, part of which is exactly to manage and reduce costs. Higher management wants to know how you will do that, not to have success at cost reduction just assumed.

The right way to select the proper subjects for budgeting assumptions is an inside out reasoning process. Don't start with generalities such as inflation or recession; you won't know how to apply the assumption after you make it. Start with the definition and planning (chapter 3) of the unit's work. From this, decide the most important factors that determine and influence unit outputs and costs. Then decide which of these output dictators and cost drivers are inherently uncertain (that is, uncontrollable). These are the subjects for which assumptions then are made.

Some examples of inherent uncertainties that may have major effects on costs and outputs of various functions, and thus are appropriate subjects for budgeting assumptions, are the following:

All functions   Prices of significant, repetitive purchase items. For example, "The price of heating oil will average 10 percent higher than this year."

Payroll   New deductions that will change payroll processing costs. For example, "The planned changes in fringe benefits will be effective on March 1."

Sales   Competitors' actions that affect revenue. For example, "ABC Company will introduce a lower-priced widget on June 1."

A caution is that assumptions are not appropriate for things to which managers are supposed to contribute. For example, an assembly unit manager is supposed to contribute to the factory production schedule. Thus, such unit managers cannot claim that the production schedule is inherently uncertain, even though they cannot control it themselves, because they are *involved* in establishing it. However, factory wage levels set by human resources—a different department—are a valid example of an important uncontrollable cost for an assembly unit manager.

Once this selection of the subjects for the assumptions is done, the numerical values—"Prices of components A, B, and C will increase 15 percent over this year; other component prices will stay the same"—or descriptive statements—"Business X will move its factory out of our area during the spring"—are your most reasonable expectations based on knowledge, experience, and thought.

How important is it that assumptions turn out to be correct? It is important that the assumptions that influence management action be reasonable, but correctness is not the point. *The reason explicit assumptions are used is that the budget must deal with future uncertainty about uncontrollable things.* If the numerical value of the assumption proves incorrect, that alerts management to the fact that conditions are then different from what was predicted, so they must react by changing actions and expectations. This identification of uncontrollables and the use of assumptions in managing and measuring are the important things, not whether the initial assumptions were correct.

Selling the Idea of Explicit Assumptions

Some companies make explicit assumptions an integral part of the budgeting process. Selection of assumption subjects and values is done early, with direct higher-management involvement so that assumptions are consistent across the company or division. Budget reviews at all levels then focus separately on the assumptions and on how the company should employ its resources. As the budget year progresses, assumptions are modified when changes in external or internal factors invalidate an assumption, and these modifications are reflected in measurement of performance against budgets.

If your company does not include explicit assumptions in its budgeting process, budgeters should still make them. Their task is more difficult, however, because they have to sell their bosses on the value of explicit assumptions in budgeting, management, and measurement. They need to sell the following assumptions:

- Particular important things about the unit's work are beyond the control of the unit.
- Unit costs and outputs may be significantly changed by changes in such inherent uncertainties (in other words, the score may be different if the rules change).
- Continual reference to, and review of, explicit assumptions is the best way to handle these inherent uncertainties.
- Budgeters should be measured on how well they manage and perform on the factors they can influence and control.

Conclusion: The Assumptions Process

1. Think through the unit's work definition and plans and select subjects for assumptions as explained in this chapter. (There will be only a small number of truly important inherent uncertainties, but these can be crucial.)
2. Make reasonable predictions for assumption values for each subject.

3. Submit these prominently as supplementary information included in the submitted budget forms.

4. In budget presentations and reviews, stress the relationship and influence of your assumptions on your various budget numbers.

5. If your boss wants an assumption changed, do it without argument. However, if challenged, vigorously defend the uncontrollability of your assumption subjects.

6. Throughout the year at performance reviews, stress how variation in values of uncontrollables have affected your costs and outputs.

3

Defining and Planning
the Work

Budgeters must understand their unit's work, not only for budgeting, but to be able to manage that work. All office professionals define their work to some extent. Doing it deliberately and completely is the best way to pave the way for good budgets and their defense.

The work definition is usually more complex than it first appears and requires some effort. It should be done before budgeting begins, because of the ever-present time pressure during the budgeting process. Fortunately, you only have to do it once, only correcting it for changes thereafter.

The proper way to define the unit's work is in terms of its outputs, inputs, and activities. Visualize your unit's work in terms of the following flow:

$$\text{Inputs} \longrightarrow \text{Activities} \longrightarrow \text{Outputs}$$

Outputs are the physical or informational things that the unit produces—product designs, assembled units, reports, paychecks, and so on. *Inputs* are the raw material, instructions, and the like, that are supplied to the unit to do its work. *Activities* are what the unit *does* to transform inputs into outputs.

Most of a unit's outputs go to other units, and most of its inputs are outputs from other units. Further, different choices of activities change the inputs required. Thus outputs, inputs, and activities are the nuts and bolts of how different units and functions work together to conduct the business, and the place where performance improvements and cost reductions are made. For a payroll unit, automation of time records (that is, different inputs) would eliminate or change review, data entry, and error correction activities. Similarly, the activity change of switching to an external payroll service would change most of the inputs that the payroll unit requires.

Each unit's work definition is different, of course, so you have to determine your own. However, we will describe general sources and categories that can guide your definition.

Activities

People tend to talk in terms of functions ("I am in sales"), but discussion in activity terms ("I make cold calls and sales presentations on products A, B, and C throughout Ohio") provides a better basis for managing the work, improving performance, predicting costs, and reducing costs. Thus, a focus on activities is the best way to define the work.

An activity is the way a business uses its resources (labor, materials, time, information, and technology) to produce particular outputs. For example, material flow in a factory can be discussed in terms of the functions involved: possibly material management, quality control, and accounting. However, those words don't tell you what you have to *do*. Much more information for managing and budgeting is contained in descriptions of the activities involved: receive material, inspect material, move material, store material, pay for material, and supply material to assembly.

The activities that a unit performs are determined by its required outputs; management decisions regarding equipment, people, processes, and procedures; and inputs.

Activities usually fall into a sort of hierarchy. In defining them, choose the level that is useful in managing and that involves significant costs. "Arrange and schedule meetings" may be a significant activity for administrative assistants, but not for their bosses. The meetings themselves might not even be significant activities for the bosses, who may see them only as a part of activities involved in integrating and controlling geographically separated subordinates.

Further, the principle of diminishing returns applies to definition of activities. The important thing is to define high-cost and highly variable activities, and to relate them to outputs. An "other" category is useful and permissible for support and incidental activities that do not vary much with output. Every organization should also have something like "administration" to cover activities like training, appraisals, and employee communication.

Outputs

There are many types of business organizations with many kinds of outputs. The *primary outputs* usually follow directly from the organization's function: assembled products from an assembly unit, orders from a sales unit, copies from a reproduction center, and products shipped from a division.

Note that revenue is not properly an organizational output. In the sense of the work to be done, revenue is a by-product of outputs such as products shipped and services delivered.

The next step must be the *specifications* that complete the description of the primary outputs. For the assembly unit, this includes specifications of the products assembled and the required quality level. For the sales unit, it includes the products sold and the geographical area or market in which they are sold.

Beyond these primary outputs, every organization has *information outputs*. The assembly unit must provide time records by project for its personnel, records of output achieved, and reports of usage and storage of toxic materials. The sales unit must report its sales calls and submit travel expense reports. The payroll unit must prepare and submit payroll tax returns. Plans, budgets, material requests, and such are required from most units.

Most organizations also have what we can call *service outputs*. They must answer inquiries, satisfy complaints, and provide expertise to sister organizations to solve problems and the like. Sales, factory, and service people all have expert advice to give on the design and features of new products.

Ordinarily, the primary outputs are the main determinants of activities and costs, but not always. In some cases, information outputs—compliance with federal environmental, safety, and tax regulations—can add considerable effort and cost. Important outputs are not necessarily only the obvious ones, which is why deliberate analysis and observation are needed.

Inputs

There are essentially three kinds of organizational inputs.

First, there are the things on which the organization operates, which we will call the *material*. These are the things that are traditionally considered inputs to any activity in the narrow definition of the term.

Second, there are things from other functions that help an organization conduct its activities. These are the *tools*, assistance or support. Examples are computer programs, candidates for employment from human resources, artwork, and physical tools and equipment.

Third, there are things that prescribe how an organization will do its work, the *instructions*. Examples are drawings, data entry procedures, bills of material, and policies and procedures.

Consider a sales unit. Its material inputs are the products and services to be sold and identification of current customers. Tool inputs can be advertising and sales promotion, proposals and quotations prepared by engineering, management visits, financing arrangements, and contract forms. Instructions include price lists and allowable terms and conditions, antitrust policies, order-entry procedures, and expense account rules for entertaining customers.

The material inputs can be physical things, such as component parts for assembly, faulty equipment for maintenance service, cash for a banking transaction, and the goods to be sold in a retail store. It can also be information, evidenced by paper or bits stored in a computer: all the activity records that are accounting's inputs, product descriptions for sales, product requirements for engineering, material requests for purchasing, signed applications for insurance rating and pricing, and so forth. In the same way, tools can be physical things or information. Instructions are always information.

Output Dictators

Once an organization's outputs are defined, you must determine what dictates those outputs, so that you will know where to look for the numbers that define next year's budget.

Some organizations have outputs dictated directly by orders, contracts, or *revenue*. This applies to an engineering organization totally devoted to customer development contracts and a service function devoted to customer maintenance contracts.

More typical are organization outputs that are dictated by *derivatives of revenue*. Factories generally have a planning function that schedules all factory operations. Assembly, test, and machine shop organizations have their outputs defined by these schedules, rather than directly by revenue. For organizations whose transactions generate revenue—cashing checks, selling a security, or switching telephone calls—the transaction itself is the output that determines the work, rather than the revenue involved.

The next logical category is *outside requirements*, independent of revenue. Legal and regulatory requirements, markets, and competition all dictate company outputs. Examples are annual and quarterly reports, compliance with environmental regulations, and proposal information that satisfies government procurement regulations.

Some outputs are dictated by *structural factors*. These dictators are a result of the physical, procedural, and organizational way in which the company does business. The way a company is organized fundamentally establishes the responsibilities and outputs of all its units. The fact of locations in a number of states and countries dictates a particular set of shipping, tax return, and communication outputs.

Finally, there are units whose outputs are dictated by requests for *service*. Their outputs are determined simply by the demands of their "customers," and they might be called *level of effort* functions. Reproduction, word processing, art departments, and parts of facilities are examples of such functions.

In practice, one organization may have outputs of all the above types. A purchasing unit in a manufacturing department can have outputs dictated by pass-through revenue, production schedules, and inventory policy; an outside requirement to report on the proportion of orders placed with small or minority businesses; and a service requirement to fulfill random headquarters purchasing needs.

Cost Drivers

Finally, the things that cause or drive the unit's costs must be understood for the unit's work to be planned and budgeted intelligently. Knowledge of cost drivers is also important in evaluating changes during the budgeting process and also changes in plans during the course of the budget year. That knowledge allows managers to understand quickly whether such changes will have major or minor effects, require quick reaction, or can be taken in stride.

Note that the most important use of knowledge of cost drivers is not in budgeting. Rather, it is in improving organizational performance. The cost drivers show where to look for the biggest improvement payoffs.

Required outputs and *output dictators* are obvious cost drivers. Usually, the more products assembled or engineering changes to be made and processed, the higher will be the costs. Also, output complexity and diversity increases costs. Changing output requirements to specify higher-performance products will increase purchased material and manufacturing costs. The characteristics of required outputs that drive cost are generally identical with the output dictators discussed in the previous section: revenue, derivatives of revenue, outside requirements, structural factors, and requests for service.

Procedures and processes, the way the work is done, is the second general class of cost drivers. Another way of saying this is that costs are driven by the choice of activities and inputs. In general, the two biggest factors that affect procedure and process cost drivers are the degree of automation and the number of things an organization does versus what it buys.

The general *price level* is also a determinant of costs, and this includes the price levels for everything an organization buys: purchased material prices, wage levels, rent levels, and so on. This type of cost driver is usually beyond the manager's control, and price changes can invalidate a budget quickly. (Price levels of important items are always candidates for budget assumptions.)

Summary and Process: Defining the Work

For an existing unit, the process of capturing the way things are currently done is neither more nor less than thorough observation and recording. When an existing unit is presented with requirements for new outputs, the process of defining the work is one of design rather than observation: Given a new output, what work (activities) will we do to accomplish it, and what inputs do we need? A new unit must define the work from scratch, and that is the manager's first task.

For all cases, use the following step-by-step process:

1. Start with the required outputs.

    Primary outputs

    Output specifications

    Information outputs

    Service outputs

Use the general categories of outputs as a checklist to ensure that nothing has been missed.

2. Determine what dictates each required output.

    Revenue

    Derivatives of revenue

Outside requirements

Structural factors

Requests for service

This helps you understand the output requirements better and tells you where to look for the amounts and values of outputs that have to be reflected in your budget.

3. Decide the way you want to do the work to produce the outputs. Define all the tasks involved in producing the outputs.

Group your conclusions into significant and manageable activities.

4. Identify the inputs needed for each of the defined activities.

What are the materials (physical or informational) that must be operated on or transformed to achieve this output?

What tools, assistance, and support are needed to do this?

What instructions are needed?

5. Iterate among outputs, inputs, and activities to determine the most practical and cost-effective way to produce the outputs. Inputs needed for preferred activities may not be available or too expensive, requiring activities to be changed. Ask the following questions:

Is there a better way to do the work?

Are there other activities and inputs that will give better performance and/or lower costs in producing the outputs?

Since your unit's outputs are another unit's inputs, are there different outputs that will improve overall company performance or reduce company costs?

6. Determine the causes or drivers of unit costs. Concentrate on those things that most strongly determine the organization's cost level. If monthly reports are an incidental cost, don't worry about what drives their costs. In identifying cost drivers, progress from the definition of activities to the nature of the costs to the drivers of those costs. That is, rather than starting with some general categories of cost drivers, look for what drives the individual cost elements: labor, purchased material, rent, utilities, and so forth.

Planning Next Year's Work

After defining the unit's work, the next step is to plan next year's work.

Everyone plans, all the time. Assume you want to go from New York to Chicago. You would not just go out your front door without any further thought. The first part of your plan would be to decide whether you want to go by plane, car, train, or bus. The answer may be quick and obvious to you, or the decision may require some work: collecting information on schedules, costs, comfort, and the like.

Assuming you decide to go by car, you would not just get into your car without further thought. You would first decide what route to take. You would decide whether to drive straight through or stop overnight on the way. In the latter case you would decide where to stop, or you may decide to make that decision when the time comes. You would decide how much money and what supplies to take with you. You would decide whether to have the car serviced.

You would probably not write all of this down, at least not in the fancy report or presentation format of a typical business plan. However, you would have decided how you were going to get to Chicago before you started the trip.

Planning is just that simple and, at the same time, just that complex. A plan must tell us how we are going to get there from here, after defining what "there" is.

The Elements of Business Planning

A business plan is the determination of the way resources will be used to achieve particular results. To do this, a plan must contain the following elements:

The *goal—a statement of the desired results to which the plan is addressed.* The goal will change as the planning progresses. In the above simple example, the goal of the first planning stage was to decide the best way to go to Chicago. That decision led to another plan whose goal was to determine the best way to go to Chicago by car.

The *"what"—everything that must be done to achieve the desired results.* In the Chicago car trip this includes choosing the route and deciding whether to stop overnight. "Choosing the route" implies an earlier activity of "getting a map." The decision of whether to stop overnight is a prerequisite to the decision of what clothes to take.

The *"how"—the methods and approaches that will be used to accomplish all the things that must be done.* In deciding how to go to Chicago, you might gather timetables and call airlines and railroads yourself, or you might give the whole task to a travel agent. For the car trip itself, the "how" would include the number of drivers and whether to take food or stop for meals.

The *"when"—the schedule for accomplishing all the activities and the final results.* For the Chicago trip, you would start with the date and time you need to be there, working back to when the various decisions must be made. Finally, with the entire plan in hand, the departure date and time would be decided.

The *"how much"—the resources required to carry out the plan: people, money, particular skills, outside purchased items, etc.* Even for the simple example of the Chicago trip, you want to know the total cost and particular things to buy, such as clothes and food.

The above items are the essential elements of any business plan. There are also supporting elements that most plans should contain. The following allow justification, evaluation, and proper modification of plans and resulting work:

- The *"why"* defense of the activities and schedules chosen to achieve the desired results.
- The *assumptions* made in the plan.
- *Contingency plans that* will be used if assumptions prove incorrect or particular activities are unsuccessful.

The Planning Work of Budgeting

This discussion of the general world of planning provides a context for the planning work of budgeting:

Goal:	To predict organization outputs, costs, and needs from other organizations
"What" and "how"	The outputs, inputs, and activities that define the organization's work for next year
"When"	Schedules of outputs, inputs, and activities
"How much"	Costs and needs from other organizations
"Why"	Justification that results in budget approval

Assumptions   Explicit budgeting assumptions
Contingency plans   Generally implicit—part of getting the budget
                     approved

In budgeting, the overall period for the plan is given: the next year. Reduced to essentials, the budgeting process asks each budgeter the question, "What outputs can your unit achieve next year at what cost, what particular resources are required, and what do you need from other units and functions?" That is the planning *goal* for unit budgeting.

The *what* and the *how* of the budget are the definition of the unit's work for next year. That definition should be done before budgeting begins, because the time pressure makes it difficult to do during budgeting. The task during budgeting, then, is to define that work for *next year*.

In addition to the work definition, the starting point is knowledge of this year's costs. Once the budgeter knows this year's work definition and costs, the planning focus for many units should be what will change: *How will next year be different from this year?* This focus applies to manufacturing units making roughly the same things from year to year, maintenance service units maintaining the same equipment, payroll and human resources units, and the like.

However, if your unit does different work each year, knowledge of this year's costs and work definition helps only as background knowledge. In an engineering unit that works on design projects, for example, each of those for next year must be defined and planned from scratch in terms of outputs, inputs, and activities.

The Planning Process

To plan next year's work in the latter case:

1. Start with analysis of the cost drivers to determine which are most important for next year. Knowing this tells the budgeter the most important outputs and activities to focus on, and the combinations of outputs, inputs, and activities whose change will yield the biggest payoffs.

2. Identify the type and amount of required outputs. Some outputs will be given to you by bosses and other functions, but most you have to dig out for yourself. The important output dictators you

defined usually dictate the places to look for output requirements, such as the following:

Production schedules for an assembly unit

Maintenance schedules for a customer service unit

Operating schedules for an operations function

Customer contracts for required reports and other compliance activities

The legal department for changes in regulations for handling toxic waste

3. Make assumptions for those outputs that are unknown, uncertain, and uncontrollable.

4. These specified and assumed outputs determine the amount and type of needed activities, and the resulting needed inputs.

5. At first, define the activities only tentatively and then check the availability of inputs and/or determine if anything has changed about familiar inputs. Then finalize activities and inputs together so they are compatible.

6. Inputs may require some temporary assumptions in the early stages of budgeting when available inputs may not be known as yet.

7. The unit's costs, determined with the help of the cost drivers, then flow directly from the activities for the given and assumed level of outputs.

8. Needs from other organizations flow from the inputs required.

The resulting schedule of all outputs, inputs, and activities is then the *when* of the budget planning. The costs and needs numbers are the *how much*.

Iterations

After your initial budget plan is put together, expect a number of iterations or "reworks" of that plan before it is finalized. The budgets of all the company's units and departments must fit together, and all must be compatible with the company's goals and strategies. Following are examples of iterations to expect—and, in some cases, to seek:

- The availability of different kinds of inputs can change the activities, or a better way to do things may be found from a different combination of inputs and activities.

- The amount and kind of required outputs may change as the budget is consolidated and reworked and as other organizations specify different needs from your unit's needs.
- The required level of outputs may not be achievable because of resource and capability limitations. Therefore, "resulting outputs" may be different from "required outputs," starting another iteration rippling through the company.

Work Definition and Planning Payoffs

- Understanding the work to be done is the *only* way that the budget can be the best prediction possible.
- They are the best defense of the budget in reviews.
- They facilitate changes required in the course of budgeting.
- During the year, they let you see cause and effect if problems arise in meeting the budget.

4

Generating the Numbers

The numbers that go into next year's budget are necessarily estimates. There is no way you can know exactly what revenues, costs, and other numbers will be next July or August.

The Kinds of Numbers

Company budgets ultimately predict amounts of profit, revenue, and cash flow, and two types of costs: (1) expenses—the day-to-day operating costs that go into the profit and loss (P&L) statement; and (2) capital expenditures—costs of investments (tools, equipment, computers, and the like) that are accumulated separately and charged to the P&L over a series of years. Company policy and accounting rules determine the costs that are "capitalized" and "expensed."

Budgeters are primarily concerned with costs (and accounting ultimately categorizes them into capital or expense). The things that make up their costs are man-hours of effort, all the various purchases needed, number of employees, etc.

In addition, various budgeters deal with other kinds of numbers, mostly unit outputs, that eventually lead to profit and cash flow, such as the following:

- Sales: orders, revenue
- Manufacturing: assemblies, fabrications, tests, shipments, revenue
- Operations: transactions of all kinds, hours of operation, service calls, revenue
- Treasury: cash receipts

In some companies, these various elements are budgeted in units of work: man-hours of effort, units assembled and shipped, units purchased, etc. Accounting then converts these into dollar amounts. In other companies, budgeters do the translation themselves, their submitted budget numbers being dollars. Our discussion will always deal with dollars; estimating work units is always involved and included in that dollar prediction.

Additionally, all these numbers are usually required by product, project, work order number, and the like. Companies want to know the profitability and cash flow of their different products and activities. Therefore, one overall number for revenue, for example, is not enough; revenue by product usually has to be budgeted.

Use Perspective in Number Generation

Major costs require extensive, intelligent analysis, because the impact of a mistake is large. If a particular line item is only 2 percent of your total budget, however, don't waste time on it. Even if you are wrong by half, it only causes a 1 percent error in your total budget. Future uncertainty does not allow your whole budget to be that accurate.

To implement that perspective, categorize outputs and costs into major, minor, or in between (which we call "substantial"). If *minor*, spend minimum time on them, possibly just using this year's number or a quick guess at next year's amount.

If *substantial*, it depends on whether the unit's work is largely repetitive from year to year or changes radically. If next year's work will be:

- *Similar* to this year's, plan and analyze next year's work for changes and use those to modify this year's data.
- *Different* from this year's, use work plans and appropriate analyses of data, trends, and equations to get the predicted numbers.

If *major*, do the best and most extensive analysis of work plans and different number sources, because the penalty for a bad prediction is large.

Sources of Budget Numbers: Data

To generate all these kinds of budget numbers, the first thing to look for is *data*: values of budget entries substantiated by specific, known information. For example, orders backlog (orders received but not yet sold) to be shipped next year is an example of valid data for a budgeter who has to predict revenue; these are specific sales that can be predicted with confidence.

Examples of budgeting items for which data can often be used directly in budgeting are revenue obtained from orders backlog, rent, salaries of personnel, costs of a mature product, costs of purchases that have firm quotations, costs of doing things that have been done before, and interest income from fixed investments.

Data do not have to be certain to be used directly in the budget. Sometimes you cannot be certain of material costs, but if known and trusted vendors say prices will stay the same, these direct data are probably still the best source of the budget number.

Misuse of Data

When valid and used appropriately, data are the best source of numerical predictions for the budget. The most common misuse is stretching data beyond the time in which they are meaningful. If materials purchase prices are unstable and you do not know the vendor, you still have data on current material costs for the product, but those data are not reliable for next year. In this case, a budget assumption must be made for next year's prices, based on the best information and analysis you can find.

Another example of stretching data is the way that some people labor to put specific customer names and dates on orders expected during next year's fourth quarter. If the order cycle (from initial expression of interest to signing the order) is six months, you cannot possibly know the specific identity of customers who will place orders a year from now. It is better to use trends or equations (perhaps including assumptions) involving such things as market size, known prospects, and number of sales calls.

Being able to fill out your budget forms entirely with data is rare. Many budget numbers are usually generated from trends or equations.

Sources of Budget Numbers: Trends

If data are not valid for direct use, *trends* are another source. A trend is the rate and direction that something has been moving. If a particular cost was $100,000, $120,000, and $140,000 in three successive years, a trend has been established of a $20,000 increase per year.

Learning curves in a factory or any repetitive operation are examples of the use of trends; it is expected that people will complete tasks faster, and thus cheaper, as they become more experienced in doing them.

Seasonal trends are also a source of budget information. Toy and ice cream businesses have obvious seasonal characteristics; many other businesses have seasonal variations just as valid. Since performance against the budget is reviewed and measured monthly, seasonal characteristics must be correctly reflected.

Precision in trend evaluation is not necessary in budgeting. It is sufficient to estimate a trend by averaging or by plotting the points and visually fitting a straight or curved line to them. If purchase prices for a certain material have increased 4, 7, 6, 3, and 7 percent in each of the last five years, it would be reasonable to say that the trend is a 5.5 percent increase per year. Since we are dealing with uncertainty, there is no value in doing the work required to define that trend precisely to a thousandth of a percent.

Always Question Trends

The use of trends to generate budget numbers carries an implicit assumption that the trend will continue. Therein lies the problem. Few trends of any kind last for years; the world changes too fast for conditions that defined the trend to stay the same. More than that, however, the formation of any trend carries no guarantee that it will continue, if changing conditions and uncontrollable factors are at work. Witness the stock market, which often seems to invalidate a trend almost as soon as there is enough data for it to be recognized.

The proper way to use trends in budgeting is always as questioned trends. If the number predicted by the trend is to be used in the budget, a deliberate conclusion must have been reached that the trend will continue. The opposite is also true: To ignore a trend, a deliberate conclusion must have been reached that the trend is no longer valid.

Orders and revenue trends are always suspicious. Cost trends are more reliable, but purchase prices are also uncontrollable, and management actions to change the way things are done invalidate trends. Seasonal trends are also subject to change if certain market characteristics change, or the market puts the products in question to different uses. If the item in question involves uncontrollable outside factors, a budget assumption should be included that either the trend will continue or change.

Sources of Budget Numbers: Equations

Budgeting *equations* are algebraic descriptions of the relationship among budget items. They are built with information, knowledge, experience, or assumptions about elements of a total item of interest. If you know the cost per man-hour and the number of man-hours expended in a project, [total cost] = [cost per man-hour] × [man-hours].

Budgeting equations must be used when the other sources cannot themselves generate a needed number. The equations are derived from work definition and planning and may use data, trends, and assumptions about both. Equations must also generally be used when budgeting new activities, for which data and trends do not exist. In this case, equations must be developed for outputs and costs from the design and analysis of the new activity. Then data and trends from related activities and general experience must be used in the equations.

Illustration: A Recruiting Unit

Consider a recruiting unit budgeter whose definition of work has yielded the conclusion that the unit's strongest cost driver is simply the number of new hires. This budgeter can use work planning to structure a simple budgeting equation:

Unit cost = [a fixed amount] + [cost per new hire]
$$\times \text{[number of new hires]}$$

Data and trends yield a good estimate of the fixed amount and the costs per new hire. There are two sources of required new hires: expansion in the company and turnover. In such a service organization, the budgeter must wait for next year's plans for the entire company before the personnel expansion number to use is known. Turnover must be anticipated from data and trends, questioned, and analyzed for changing conditions. (This is a prime example of a unit's costs being determined by factors beyond the manager's control, and budget assumptions should be included for division personnel increases and turnover rates.)

Misuse of Equations

Misuse of equations in budgeting can be caused by using the wrong equations, of course—by not properly relating cause and effect. Truly understanding the drivers and dictators of outputs and costs through work definition and planning is the best antidote. There is no substitute for budgeters understanding their units' work. The other most prominent misuse is not using equations enough, that is, using direct data and trends beyond the time for which they are valid.

Budgeting Outputs

Revenue budgeting varies greatly across different kinds of businesses. Many retail businesses, for example, are *cash businesses in which revenue is made up of many small sales.* Data on individual customers are meaningless. Data or trends on past and current month-by-month sales (revenue) may be useful, but their applicability must be questioned. For example, the opening or closing of a large factory nearby is a new condition that changes the sales trend for many retail businesses. Revenue is often predicted from equations or statistical models of the served market.

Businesses that respond to orders have a different revenue budgeting problem. An order is an agreement to buy something at a specified future time and price and often implies that work must be done before delivery (for example, construction projects, military systems). For such businesses, backlog (orders received but not yet delivered) is confident data that can be used directly. Orders prospects are budgeting data if confidence in an eventual order is high. Beyond identified prospects, trends and equations (or market models) are usually the best sources.

Businesses that rely on a few large orders (such as airplane manufacturers) have a particularly difficult time budgeting revenue, because single orders are so important. Trends and statistical models are no help, because so few prospects are involved. Data from backlog and confident orders prospects are useful in budgeting. Otherwise, budgeted revenue must come from analysis of a relatively small number of individual customers.

Beyond costs and revenue, other budget numbers that have to be generated are primarily *unit outputs*: shipments, assemblies, transactions, service calls, and so on. If such outputs are directly customer driven (like bank loan closings or some kinds of customer service calls), they are predicted like revenue. If they are internally driven (like assemblies or shipments), numbers come from the work plans and all three number sources, as appropriate. For example:

- Shipments or cash receipts would be entered as data from production and revenue or collection plans.

- Numbers of assemblies could be obtained from learning curve trends.

- Assemblies could also be obtained from equations involving number of assemblers, assembly operations, and time per operation.

Budgeting Costs

A number of costs are always directly predictable from data. Rent is an example. Costs of most things that have been done before are in this category, such as mature product assembly, restaurant personnel costs, tax return preparation. Things that change slowly, such as office supplies and payroll costs, should be adequately predictable from data. Things that are bought in predictable amounts at established prices become usable data as soon as the price is known: utilities, taxes, audit fees, and so on. Where valid data are in hand, it should always be used.

Trends are valuable for predicting the costs of controllable things, but trends in the pertinent outside environment must be analyzed and questioned. Learning curves of all kinds are examples of the former. The cost of fuel for an airline is an example of the latter; oil prices change quickly, and recent data can be useless as a predictor. Things such as fuel cost are candidates for budget assumptions.

Equations come into play when data or trends do not directly yield the item needed, as when predicting costs for new activities and finding new ways to do old activities. When automation is to be substituted for labor, for example, cost equations for the automated approach are the usual and proper way to justify the expenditure involved.

The other "anchor" for next year's cost predictions is to use the best information available. Let's discuss this separately for personnel and purchase costs.

Estimating Personnel Costs

Personnel costs are labor and employee benefits. Labor costs are salaries, wages, commissions, bonuses, and such things as overtime premiums, if applicable. Benefits are vacation and holiday pay, sick pay, insurance, and the like. Conventionally, if outside contractors are used to accomplish work, rather than employees, that is a purchase cost.

There are two aspects of personnel costs to discuss: the work to be done and the costs of the employees. The first step is to predict the work to be done in terms of the number of people required, or the man-hours (or man-days) of effort required. The result is often requirements for hiring new people or for laying off current employees. Then the number of people or the man-hours effort times the predicted salaries (or direct labor rates) and fringe benefits equals the personnel cost.

Part of the prediction of the work to be done is easy, part difficult. The effort required to do repetitive tasks that have been done before, in the same way, is easy to predict. There are direct data available.

Doing old tasks in a new way is the first degree of difficulty. The new activities have to be planned, and the new effort required follows directly from that planning.

More difficult is the estimation of the effort required to do new tasks or new projects. Again, the planning and definition of the work to be done (the activities) are the bases for estimating the man-hours of effort or the number of people required. If the new task involves new, unfamiliar activities, they must be estimated from knowledge of similar work. If no one has such knowledge and experience, the new activities must be divided into elements to which knowledge and experience can be applied.

Consider a bank installing its first automatic teller machines. With no direct data, how does it budget the personnel costs for servicing and maintaining the machines? Possibly a consultant, or a new employee with experience elsewhere, can supply direct knowledge and experience. Otherwise the planning must break down the service and maintenance into familiar activities, such as counting and stocking currency, preventive maintenance on electronic and electromechanical devices, and monitoring computer transactions.

Estimating Purchase Costs

For things that are bought, the simplest costs to estimate are those bought at *known price and quantity*. Items with price labels, price lists, and catalogs are in this category. Simple, reliable data are available as the basis for next year's cost estimate. Known forthcoming price changes are also simple and reliable data.

Next to catalog items in simplicity to predict are things for which *firm quotations* are in hand. Firm quotations from suppliers are the only fully accurate way to cost the things bought for new products or activities. Firm quotations are data and should be used as such.

Sometimes firm quotations cannot be obtained, and the best information available is a *vendor estimate*, sometimes called a "budgetary quotation." In most situations, this estimate is the best data available, and the manager's cost estimate should be based on it. Again, however, judgment must be applied, because that estimate does not represent a binding commitment on the part of the vendor. As usual, all sources of information should be used: vendor past reliability, analyzed trends, estimates from multiple vendors, industry intelligence, and so forth.

Finally, there are *known things whose quantity and price will vary*, such as future utility rates, food for a restaurant, and various commodities. Such predictions are always judgments, and the experience of the right operating and purchasing people is often the best guide for these judgments. If important, these are always candidates for budget assumptions.

Cost Relationships

Every unit has costs that are related to other costs. Budgeters must understand these relationships so they don't kid themselves about what their real costs will be.

In some cases, a first cost automatically gives rise to a second kind of cost. For example, the cost of high-priced professional people necessarily includes costs of things that keep them current in their professions, such as memberships, seminars, courses, books, and magazines. If the business needs these professional people, management must accept that such supporting expenses are necessary costs of doing business.

In other cases, some costs unavoidably increase if others are cut. Further, if the current way of doing things is the most efficient way, total costs will increase if one of the cost elements is arbitrarily cut. For example, if the amount of work stays the same, employee reductions must be made up by using outside contractors or higher overtime costs. As another example, if there is a given amount of remote work to be done—selling, customer contact, working with project partners, dealing with a department in a distant city, etc.—travel and telecommunications expense cannot both be reduced. If managers cut travel expense, they must expect telecommunications expense to increase.

The only ways to cut costs are to find more efficient ways to do a given amount of work or to do less work. Budgeters need to guard against the illusion that cutting one element of cost X dollars will produce X dollars overall saving, if the work is not changed.

As usual, the specifics of such relationships are unique for each unit and have to be learned from definition and an understanding of the work.

5

Getting the Budget Approved

Developing good budgets is of no benefit if budgeters cannot get them approved. While expressed as numbers of dollars for different kinds of costs and outputs, budget approval really means the acceptance and authorization of the plans for next year, including the following:

- Expected and committed results
- Resources required to achieve the results
- Needed capital investments
- Action programs to generate outputs, improve performance, and reduce costs
- Support and inputs required from other organizational elements

Getting the right budget approved is not a trivial task. It is a selling job—the "customers" being the bosses—involving a set of objective and subjective factors like any other selling job.

Before discussing how to maximize approval probability, let's review what we have said about budgeting and the work it requires.

Review of Budgeting

Company budgets are the financial expression of company plans for next year. They are the sum of all the budgets of company component organizations, suitably transformed by accounting into higher management and financial reporting terms.

Unit budgets are not done, or approved, in a vacuum. They must reflect company strategies and plans, management priorities, and the needs and desires of interfacing organizations. Outputs to and needs from other organizations are defined in the process of planning the work and given value when generating the numbers.

The planning work of budgeting defines, for next year, the organization's outputs (which are usually inputs to other organizations), costs, and needs (inputs) from other organizations. The timing and schedules of all of these factors must be included. The proper way to define the work is in terms of outputs, activities, and inputs, together with the things that dictate the outputs and drive the costs.

Next year's outputs and inputs are never fully known at budget time. The planning must reflect that uncertainty with estimates from the best information available and explicit assumptions for those things that are uncontrollable.

In generating the budget numbers, unit budgeters primarily predict costs, but some also budget revenue and various kinds of outputs. The budget numbers flow directly from the unit work plan: the outputs, costs, needs from other organizations, and schedules. The sources of budget numbers in all prediction areas are data, trends, and equations. Explicit assumptions should supply the numbers for uncontrollable items for which none of the sources is available.

Personnel costs are predicted from work plans and wage and salary information. If possible, purchase costs are predicted from published prices and firm quotations. When that is impossible, the best data, trends, and knowledge must be used.

Getting the Work Done

The key to getting all this budgeting work done is to *recognize the severe time pressure* inherent in most company budgeting processes. Once budgeting begins, budgeters can be overwhelmed by urgent information gathering and number crunching. Budgeters should do the following before the company's budgeting process begins:

- Learn the company's budgeting process, forms, terminology, and relevant accounting usage. The best sources are accounting and your boss.

- Learn everything you can about your boss's priorities, company and division strategies and plans, accounting's priorities and points of emphasis, and the business environment and financial constraints in which the company expects to operate next year.

This will never be found on one piece of paper, but must result from extensive reading and continuing discussions with bosses, accounting people, and marketing people.

- Define the organization's current work and known forthcoming changes, in terms of outputs, inputs, activities, output dictators, and cost drivers.

- Program your budget forms onto a spreadsheet in your personal computer, for later ease of manipulation and modification.

The scheduling of this prebudgeting work depends on the situation. The important thing is to have it all completed when the company's budgeting process begins. If being done for the first time, start at least a couple of months before budgeting begins, given that this has to be a part-time activity.

During budget generation, initial concentration should be on obtaining missing information regarding required outputs and inputs; communicating with interfacing organizations concerning needs and desires back and forth; and finalizing budget assumptions, when needed information on required outputs and inputs becomes available. Then the planning and prediction of all the cost and output numbers proceed, as discussed in chapters 3 and 4.

Continuous communication is important. The budget cannot be done in a vacuum. For the company to succeed, all organization budgets must be consistent and complementary. The budget is worthless if top management strategy calls for equal emphasis on widgets and gadgets, sales budgets orders for 10,000 widgets and only 100 gadgets, and manufacturing plans to build 2,000 widgets and 8,000 gadgets. Most inconsistencies are not that obvious, but they do not have to be to have bad effects on company success.

This process uses data where possible, trends where valid, and equations and assumptions for the rest of the predictions. It uses all pertinent information about the company, the unit, and next year as soon as that information is available. The result will be a budget with the best possible prediction of next year's numbers, given the inherent uncertainty of the future.

Budget Approval

We are now ready to discuss our final topic: getting the right budget approved. We can identify three factors that affect the approval. *Objective* factors are the independent reality and logic of the submitted budget relative to the job to be done. *Environmental* refers to situational factors outside the budget itself, such as company financial health. *Psychological* refers to subjective factors involved. All three are roughly equal in importance.

Objective Factors

Not surprisingly, the first requirements of the objective aspects of getting budget approval are to have *justifications for all numbers and forceful arguments for all proposed courses of action.* Give the budget a logical basis by planning the work and generating the numbers as explained in this book.

In such a firm grounding, assumptions are particularly important and useful in the approval process. Budgeters should always be willing to change assumption values if their bosses so wish; the key point is to get the boss's agreement that the item in question *is* an appropriate assumption, i.e., uncontrollable by the budgeter and therefore something on which he or she should not be measured.

Additionally, there are personal characteristics that facilitate the objective aspects of budget approval.

Credibility. It is difficult to overemphasize the importance of a person's building a reputation for doing what he or she has promised. Many business plans and proposals are difficult to evaluate objectively; the proposer often knows more about the subject than the reviewers. This is generally true of budgets; if you say you need ten people to do something new, the boss seldom has firm data and knowledge to dispute your estimates. Your past record in being right and accomplishing things as promised can thus carry heavier weight than anything else in the boss's evaluation.

Good Presentation. The presentation should be accurate, clear, well supported, and to the point. Always keep in mind that the purpose of budget presentations is to *sell.* Neither assume it will be accepted without supporting arguments nor drown the listener in extraneous data.

Numerical and typographical errors on presentation aids are interesting examples of credibility at work. Most bosses will accept one or two such errors without effect. Have a few more such errors and the boss will conclude that you are sloppy. However, too many (and each boss has his or her own threshold) will make the boss conclude that you do not know what you are talking about. Are not such easily corrected errors a silly way to lose credibility with the boss?

Good Answers. The final important personal characteristic is having ready and lucid answers to the questions that arise. Here there is no substitute for knowledge of your job and of how the boss and other reviewers react to things. What are their "hot buttons," current problems, and priorities? Every budget submission and presentation should be reviewed beforehand for anticipated questions, and submitters should make sure that they have good answers ready.

Environmental Factors

Assume that top management decides to "run out" a certain line of business, investing no more money in it but working to obtain all cash possible before it ends. Now assume that the crusading sales manager for that business line submits a budget that doubles the sales effort for next year, in the belief that this business can be saved and made to grow again. That sales manager will undoubtedly have his head handed to him at the first budget review. He ignored an important factor when he developed his budget: Top management has decided not to invest for growth.

This is an example of the environmental aspects of budget approval at work. Environmental factors that can affect budget approval include at least the following:

- The financial condition of the company or division
- The state of the relevant outside environments: economy, market, competition, and government regulation
- The current reputation and job security of the boss and his or her bosses
- Company and division strategy and plans, particularly those regarding growth or de-emphasis of activities in which the given unit is involved.

Unfortunately, budgeters often cannot know all of the pertinent environmental factors. So what should they do?

As usual, communicate, communicate, communicate. Listen to what the boss and higher management say and watch closely what they do. Do not wait until budget submission to check an observation with the boss; do it early in the process so that you will be on the same page with him or her.

Pay strict attention to the environmental factors that you know are true, such as a bad economy, cancellation of company credit lines, or aggressive behavior by the competition. Budget accordingly:

- Any optional aggressive growth initiatives should ordinarily be proposed in good times.

- Cost reductions and productivity improvements should be emphasized in bad times.

However, never let environmental factors overwhelm the objective aspects of your planning. If confident that new equipment will have a good payoff in reduced cost or improved performance, never fail to propose it in the budget because of perceived negative environmental factors. Even if they disapprove because of hard times, you want the bosses to know about your idea.

Never do illogical budgeting because of perceived but unknown environmental factors. If you are convinced that you need more resources next year, never cut costs in the budget just because you believe (without confirmation) that is what management wants. Think of the consequences if you are wrong.

Finally, ignore the gossip about environmental factors that cannot be confirmed. Concentrate only on what is best for your organization, your boss's organization, and interfacing functions. The worst thing that can happen is that you will be sent back to redo the budget. You will not lose points for persuasively pushing what is best for your part of the company, despite a contrary indicator that you could not be expected to know.

The Psychological Factors

The psychological nature of budgeting follows unavoidably from:

- The conflict in objectives in which the boss wants the best results possible and the unit to be challenged, while the submitting unit budgeter (the subordinate) wants a budget that can be beaten.
- The fact that both boss and subordinate are dealing with uncertainty. Neither knows what the future will hold, or even exactly what resources they will need to do a specified job.

With these contradictory objectives plus the uncertainty, both boss and subordinate go through a mental process of estimating the other's state of mind.

Subordinates must begin the thought process with good budget content, so that they know the allowable limits of the forthcoming negotiation with their bosses. After that, the first question is, How will the boss react to these numbers? Budgeters should think about the boss's attitude generally, reaction to past budgets, what the boss has said or done lately, and current pressures. Budgeters should also judge how smart the boss is, where he or she can be fooled, and where the subordinate had better not try to fool him or her. The distillation of all such thinking determines the transition from what the budgeter thinks is a realistic budget to the "padded" budget that actually should be submitted.

Bosses also get a turn, of course, and they have the advantage because they are in the controlling position and are reacting rather than initiating. Bosses consider whether the subordinates are optimists or pessimists, their record in meeting commitments, whether they are polished game players, their knowledge of the situation, and general intelligence. The boss usually has a preconceived idea of approximately what the subordinate's budget should be, and this is ordinarily modified somewhat by good subordinate input.

Boss and subordinate eventually arrive at an agreed budget, with which each has varying degrees of comfort. (As in any negotiation, the result is probably better if both sides have roughly an equal degree of discomfort.)

How should the budgeter, armed with good plans for next year's work and good budget numbers, play this psychological game? It depends on the budgeter's boss and the relationship between budgeter and boss.

The best situation is the one that allows the budgeter to be straightforward and objective. If the boss is competent and reasonable and the relationship is good, this is the recommended approach. The subordinate's cost estimates, after all, are intellectually grounded, not emotional. The best budget will result if the arguments are about specific outputs, activities, inputs, or assumptions. These are the arguments that bosses and subordinates are supposed to have, and they and the company will be better off if these are the arguments joined in budget negotiations.

However, if the conditions of a good relationship with a good boss are not present, budgeters must protect themselves. They should still base their arguments on the planning and definition of their work and associated assumptions. However, it is difficult to overcome emotion with logic. If subordinates believe their budgets will be subject to emotional attack (and if they do not know, this is the safest assumption to make), they should "pad" their budgets discreetly and cleverly as a defense against emotion and arbitrary cuts.

Such padding is the enemy of good budgeting, but *the budgeter's first responsibility is to get approval of the resources needed to do next year's required work*. It is seldom as simple as adding 5 percent to everything because the boss is known to make 5 percent arbitrary cuts. It usually takes all the intelligence and perception that the budgeter can bring to bear.

Selling Your Budget

In short, the best basis for getting your budget approved is concentrated attention to the following:

- Proper intellectual grounding of the budget in the organization work plan, and the use of the best sources for budget numbers
- A good reputation and good presentations
- Appropriate attention to environmental factors
- Skilled playing of the psychological games
- Close and continual communication with the boss

The obvious, gross basis for the last requirement is that one of the worst things you can do is surprise the boss unpleasantly at budget time. That is almost guaranteed to make the budget negotiation emotional. However, a basis that is just as important is that the boss will understand your budget because the boss was privy to your reasoning as it developed. You will understand the boss's state of mind and the degree of approval or disapproval of various items before budget reviews begin.

Unfortunately, practicing powerful budgeting as described in this book cannot guarantee budget approval. The psychological world of budgeting can be full of surprises, and the pertinent environmental factors can never be fully known. Still, the recommended work will give you the best chance for approval and also put you in the best possible position to react to any surprises that the budget process brings.

Part II

Effective Purchasing

6

Understanding Purchasing

Purchasing is a major business activity that affects the entire business and involves shared responsibilities among purchasing professionals, operating people, and finance.

The most common purchasing activities of office professionals are as the users and specifiers of office-related purchases (such as copiers, desktop computers, and supplies) or as the implementers and coordinators of the needs of management specifiers (in engineering, production, facilities, etc.). However, in small companies with no purchasing function, the office professionals may do the actual buying.

Thus, office professionals either specify and use purchases or actually buy them, in either case having a role in making the company's purchasing effective and efficient. In addition to knowing how buying is done, understanding purchasing's place in the business will help them carry out that role.

Accordingly, chapter 6 starts with a general discussion of what purchasing is and how it is done followed in chapter 7 by a definition of the requirements and resulting tradeoffs that company managements need from their purchasing activity.

Chapters 8 and 9 present the activities and practices that satisfy these requirements. Chapter 8 covers the "structural" needs of knowing purchase costs, buying the items with the right performance and quality, and protecting purchasing work and assets. Chapter 9 completes the coverage of purchasing by tackling the "foundation" need: achieving the lowest possible cost consistent with the structural needs plus the quantity and time constraints.

Its Importance

Together with employee costs, purchases are where companies spend most of their money. In fact, excluding software and service companies, most businesses spend considerably more on purchases than on employee costs. In these days of automated operation, purchases may account for more than 75 percent of the operating costs of some manufacturers, distributors, and retailers.

More importantly, purchase costs are generally the place where unpleasant surprises are found and where control of costs is most easily lost. In the short term, at least, employee costs are predictable and relatively fixed. However, purchase costs can vary widely. A factory may buy too much inventory or the wrong components. A wholesaler or retailer may stock up on items that do not sell. A company may stay with a comfortable vendor, even as it keeps raising its prices. A construction company may order material to get a jump on a tough, promised project, only to have the customer change its mind before signing a contract.

Couple such surprises with the size of the purchase expense, and ineffective purchasing can quickly ruin a business year.

What Businesses Buy

Businesses ordinarily spend the most purchasing money on items directly related to revenue. In retail and distribution businesses, the things sold are generally identical to the things bought. The same thing is true of banks and insurance companies, which primarily buy and sell money.

In manufacturing businesses, raw materials, components, and subassemblies are bought and turned into products by labor. In utilities, systems and equipment and either fuel, power, or raw materials are bought and turned into delivered commodities (electricity, gas, water, etc.) through labor. For maintenance service businesses, the comparable things bought are tools and replacement parts.

These various things bought that are directly related to revenue have different names in different businesses. The most common term in manufacturing businesses is *direct material*. In retailing and distribution, they are usually called *inventory* or *stock*. The money that a bank buys is its capital and liabilities.

Most companies also buy things that are investments necessary to produce revenue or generally to conduct business. These include factory and store equipment, buildings or improvements to leased facilities, tools, computers, trucks. These are ordinarily accounted for as *capital expenditures*, budgeted and recorded separately.

Then there are a wide variety of other things that businesses buy, including advertising, freight services, consultants, legal services, temporary personnel, subscriptions and training courses for employees, and facilities-related things like space (rent), utilities, security guards, repair, and maintenance.

How Businesses Buy

Most commonly, the user or specifier of needed goods or services directs a *purchase request*, or *material request*, to the purchasing function. The output of the purchasing function is then a *purchase order* to a vendor, specifying everything necessary to obtain the goods or services in question. Upon receipt of goods, a receiving function or the user inspects them for purchase order fulfillment. Finally, finance decides when and how to pay, and pays, vendors' invoices for accepted purchases. Finance also ordinarily decides whether needed items are bought or leased.

The user/specifier (in operations, marketing, engineering, production planning, etc.) states *what* is needed and *when* it is needed in the purchase request. The purchasing professional determines *how* it is bought, from *whom* and *where*, and for *how much*. Purchasing also determines *when*, in the sense of the time that ordering and delivery should take place to have the right amount on hand when the specifier needs it. All of this information is reflected in the purchase order.

Modifications and Constraints

The typical purchasing authority to select the vendor, however, is constrained in a number of ways. Sometimes the user, purchasing, and finance limit potential vendors through a vendor certification process. This approves vendors for supply of particular items, and also implies possible decertification for poor performance. Certification includes visits to vendor facilities and study of information to evaluate adequacy and care of production equipment, personnel skill and technical knowledge, means of ensuring and controlling quality, and management competence, as well as financial health.

Another common constraint on purchasing authority is multiple sourcing, in which the total need for a particular item is divided among two or more suppliers. Used by the federal government and some companies for important items, it protects against poor performance or outright failure by one supplier. The downside is that multiple sourcing often increases costs and purchasing effort.

There are other ways that purchasing responsibilities and processes vary widely. For example, engineering may specify a particular part in a product design, available from only one vendor. In such a case, the purchasing professionals obviously do not have the vendor selection responsibility and have little range for price negotiation. Then there are extremes in which the typical process hardly applies.

The Extremes

At one extreme is a consulting contract. A manager needs help with something, and the work specification may be little more than "Investigate area X for two months and make written recommendations." The manager who wants the consulting services ordinarily specifies everything, including who will do the work at what price over what time period. Many companies do not require a formal purchase request in this case. The purchasing professional is involved only in the form of the consulting contract and is mainly concerned only with legally protecting the company.

At the other extreme is a major contract on a construction or military systems project. In this case, "who," "what," "when," and "how" are top management decisions, usually with marketing as well as operational considerations. Here a complex contract replaces the purchase order; and specification, negotiation, and contract administration can each be a major task. For large projects, a dedicated contract organization may administer the entire process, with most of the content specification coming from engineering and general management.

Discussion of so many variations and extremes may seem to downgrade the importance of "most commonly" that was originally described. The truth is that most companies use the common practice for most purchases, but office professionals should understand that there are exceptions, and good reasons for them.

How Businesses Organize Their Buying

Giant companies typically have purchasing organizations in each of their divisions and probably have a corporate staff function that promotes the advantages of common buying for some things across the entire company. Large and middle-sized companies may have one centralized purchasing organization, or may have decentralized purchasing into each operation, location, or department, depending usually on the nature of the business. Smaller companies generally have one purchasing organization.

In manufacturing companies, purchasing is usually a part of the manufacturing department, because manufacturing is the specifier and user of most of the purchases. In other kinds of businesses, the purchasing manager may report to operations, finance, or administration.

The question of whether to have one purchasing organization or many is a standard centralization versus decentralization tradeoff: Centralization promotes competence and minimum cost, but possibly at the unacceptable risk of insufficient understanding and responsiveness to the user activities served. The best solution is often decentralized buying plus a mechanism—another organization, higher management, committee, or task force—to certify vendors, select purchase items, and standardize both across the company for common items.

Very small companies may not have purchasing organizations at all, assigning office professionals do the buying, sometimes independently, for different locations and activities. Adding a professional buyer clearly increases employee costs immediately, but may reduce purchase costs through standardization, increased effort and attention, and higher purchasing knowledge and competence. The best answer depends on the company and is a major decision for a small company president.

7

Defining the Requirements and Tradeoffs

What does company management need from its purchasing activity? Because management wants the highest profit possible, it may seem that the need is only to

Buy everything at the lowest cost.

Oh, if business life were only that simple. There are many other requirements on a company's purchasing activity, and some of them seem contradictory. That is, like everything else in business, there are major tradeoffs. Let's build the requirements and probe these tradeoffs.

First, the company must buy the right things. Every manufacturing part must "fit" with all other parts in all its characteristics: size, shape, perhaps voltage or fluid capacity, strength, and so on. Purchased items must have the performance that satisfies the purpose for which they were bought. The cheapest copier is not the right copier if it does not fulfill the office's copying requirements.

Second, they must be at the right quality. This is usually neither the highest nor lowest quality, but rather the quality that matches the function of the items or the target market of a resulting product. And management wants that function to be carried out, or that product produced, at the lowest possible cost. The requirement for adequate performance and quality at the lowest possible cost defines the first major purchasing tradeoff.

Tradeoff: Performance vs. Quality vs. Price

From time to time, the press loves to flay the government for items like alleged $700 hammers and $1,000 toilet seats. Conservative engineers sometimes specify components with more than twice the needed rating, or capability, just to be safe. Some offices insist on an expensive brand of copy paper, when most paper salespeople will tell you that all copy papers of a given weight are essentially the same.

These are all examples of specifying higher performance or quality than needed, and all result in paying a higher price than necessary.

The Economic Realities

If you had unlimited funds to build a house that you expected your family and descendants to occupy for a hundred years, you would specify the best possible materials, construction, fixtures, and appliances. Everything would be "top of the line." However, that is not the reality of modern life. Instead, you would try to specify the best house that you could afford with the features that you want the most, while keeping one eye on things that enhance or degrade resale value.

All businesses face similar economic realities. Products are specified for price and performance aimed at particular markets. No one expects a compact car to have the performance, features, or reliability of a Mercedes. Purchasing the "right" things seldom means the "highest" quality. Except for lowest-end products, it also seldom means the "cheapest" price. Rather, designers must trade off performance, quality, and price to specify the items that match the intent of the product.

The same thing applies to nonproduct purchases. Giant companies and large banks conclude that expensive headquarters facilities and furniture, perhaps even collections of fine art, are important and justified for their corporate image. The same expenditures would be totally inappropriate for a small manufacturing company.

Applying That Reality to the Business Office

To bring this discussion into the business office, the whole structure of the computer industry makes it difficult to buy the "right" desktop computers, for example. It currently makes sense to standardize desktop computers and software within a company, and companies then tend to install almost all the software on all computers. From one point of view, this puts all company functions into position to benefit from increased computerization of their work. From another point of view, however, much of this potential capability represents "junk" that only slows operation on the few tasks performed on a given computer.

A set of database and spreadsheet capabilities facilitates inventory control, and things such as graphics and multiple fonts facilitate desktop publishing of sales literature. However, many employees use their computers—more effectively and efficiently, surely—for only the same things they formerly did with typewriters. In this sense, it is a shame that the personal computer industry moved away from its early emphasis on word processors, which would cost-effectively satisfy most "typists," at both lower cost and less aggravation.

Thus, the computer industry now makes it difficult to buy the most efficient and effective computers for every function because it sells general purpose desktops. However, at least companies can choose the cheaper models with less memory and less software for the users that do little more than type.

Here are some other performance/quality/cost tradeoffs in the business office:

- Copier needs are most basically determined by the number of copies made per day or month. A lot of money is wasted on a copier designed and priced for 30,000 copies per month for an office that only makes 1,000. Features such as copying both sides of a paper also waste money unless such "duplexing" is a frequent requirement. How much effort is it, after all, to separately copy each side of a page once in a while?

- For internal use, expensive copy paper is a waste. However, it may make sense for marketing materials sent outside the company.

- Overnight mail is useful, but some offices make it a habit. Regular mail is adequate for most business information. On the other hand, overnight mail may be worth the extra cost if one wishes to convey a sense of urgency or responsiveness.

- Three-color printing on forms, envelopes, and stationery sent outside the company may make sense, but not on those used internally.

Adding to the Basic Requirement

The first additions to "buy everything at the lowest cost" thus change that basic requirement to

Buy *the right things* at the lowest possible cost, *consistent with adequate performance and quality.*

But we are far from finished. The next addition is that the right quantity must be ordered at the right time. Clearly, the right amount must be on hand when needed. Beyond this simple statement, however, lies the second major tradeoff.

Tradeoff: The Right Quantity vs. Price vs. Time

The price of almost all manufactured goods, printing, and some ser-vices, varies inversely with the order quantity—the bigger the order, the lower the unit price. At first blush, this says that companies should buy the largest quantity of everything they are confident that they will use, limited only by available storage space and shelf life of various items. Further, it would seem that these large quantities should be bought as soon as the need is apparent, so there will never be any shortages.

However, all those purchases represent an investment until they are used. Of all the financial performance criteria, a company's return on its investment is arguably the most important. Further, if most of the company's cash is tied up in materials sitting on shelves, at some point it will not be able to attack opportunities or problems that arise.

The Tradeoff Is Always Financial

Thus, there is always a tradeoff between buying at the lowest price (for given performance and quality) and minimizing investment. This trade-off is expressed and resolved financially. Return on investment equals profit divided by investment. The lower prices from large quantity or-ders increase profit, but also investment. To be rigorous, related costs should be included—large, infrequent purchases require more storage space but less purchasing effort, for example—but these are often small compared to the profit and investment effects. (Of course, all bets are off if a company buys material that is never used, such as components for a product that is then discontinued or a year's supply of printer ink cartridges just before new models are bought.)

In practice and for good reasons, the tradeoff analysis is different for revenue-producing items than for all other purchases. For the former, the best tradeoff resolution is usually to keep as little as possible on hand. For the latter, it usually pays to buy the largest quantity consis-tent with available storage space and potential that needs will change. As an example of changing needs, the potential for telephone area code changes has recently become a real limiting factor in the pur-chase amounts of stationery and business forms.

Non-Revenue-Producing Purchases

Taking non-revenue-producing purchases first, assume that a com-pany buys copy paper every month (we have to pick some reasonable minimum—no one is going to order a day's worth of copy paper every day). The company learns that the price per carton of a year's supply is 20 percent cheaper than for a month's supply. Assume that plenty of air-conditioned storage space is available. (This space is free at least in terms of out-of-pocket costs. All bets are again off if someone decides to rent more space just to store copy paper.) Should the company buy the year's supply?

A simple and sufficiently accurate comparison resolves the tradeoff: the company's cost of money versus the savings of buying the larger quantity. If the savings are greater, buying the larger quantity makes sense. The cost of money is the interest rate at which the company can borrow multiplied by the time the money is tied up. Assume that this company's annual interest rate is 10 percent. Since we are comparing a purchase now with monthly purchases across the year, the average time that the money is tied up is about six months, so the related cost of money is half the annual rate, or 5 percent. Clearly, buying the annual quantity at a 20 percent saving is economical; the company could even borrow money to do it and come out ahead.

Printing is a good illustration of other considerations that go into the buying quantity decision. Printing is an extreme case of quantity lowering unit price. The cost of printing is mostly in the setup, not the production, so 3,000 copies of a business form may cost just a few dollars more than 1,000 copies. Buy as much as you can store, right? Not exactly. First, the form may change. Second, forms in storage may be damaged. And so on. The result is that it neither makes sense to buy a month's nor a two years' supply, and people usually consider about a six months' supply to be the best amount to buy.

Revenue-Producing Purchases

The natural tendency for production managers is to buy enough factory components, as soon as possible, so the factory never has work stoppages due to parts shortages. Similarly, store managers would like to buy enough stock, as soon as possible, so the store never loses a sale for lack of product.

However, they are both paid primarily to maximize return on investment. That is, the production manager is responsible for maximizing production with the smallest inventory possible, and the store manager is responsible for maximizing sales on the smallest inventory (stock) possible.

Thus, the tradeoff:

- Buy too much too soon, and money needed for other things is tied up in material sitting on shelves. At best, this lowers return on investment. At worst, it drives the company into bankruptcy.

- Buy too little too late, and operations slow or stop. Lack of factory material slows or stops production, and lack of store stock reduces sales; both thus reduce profit.

Keeping the dollar numbers small for simplicity, consider a confident store that buys $1,000 worth of products in January and sells them in equal amounts over the next five months at 100 percent markup (that is, products that cost the store $1,000 are sold for $2,000). The following table shows the cash flow from the products for six months. Amounts are in dollars. Cash flow equals sales minus purchases in this simple example. Cum. (cumulative) cash flow is the algebraic sum of cash flows through the given month:

Months	Jan.	Feb.	March	April	May	June	Total
Purchases	1000						1000
Sales	0	400	400	400	400	400	2000
Cash flow	−1000	400	400	400	400	400	1000
Cum. cash flow	−1000	−600	−200	200	600	1000	

Now consider the same sales, but with the store buying a month's worth of inventory every month, starting in January:

Months	Jan.	Feb.	March	April	May	June	Total
Purchases	200	200	200	200	200	0	1000
Sales	0	400	400	400	400	400	2000
Cash flow	−200	200	200	200	200	400	1000
Cum. cash flow	−200	0	200	400	600	1000	

This illustration is oversimplified, but realistic enough to show the large payoff from buying inventory only when needed. Look at the cumulative cash flow. The same cash—$1,000—is generated in six months in both cases, but the first case required a $1,000 investment (that is, maximum negative cumulative cash flow), while the second required $200. If the store buys everything month-to-month instead of at the beginning of the year, it can stock five times as much product to sell.

Even if stretching the purchases increases their costs, the second way is usually better. If purchase cost increases 20 percent, for example, to $240 per month for a total of $1,200, cumulative cash flow in June is $800 for an investment in January of $240, still much better than the first case ($1,000 cash for $1,000 investment).

Similarly, some lost sales because of lack of stock would not make the second case worse than the first. However, this is the place where management judgment comes in: stores must buy enough, quickly enough, that lost sales do not become a major problem. This is the familiar management balancing act of trying to buy just enough product to avoid major problems, while tolerating some minor problems in the interest of greater return on investment.

While different in specifics, the same reasoning applies to production managers, distributors, and any business that buys revenue-producing materials.

Modifying the Basic Requirement Again

By now it is clear that the "lowest possible cost" does not necessarily mean buying at the cheapest price. Previously, we saw that the right performance and quality make the "right" price often differ from the cheapest price. Now, we have seen that minimizing investment, as well as limits on storage space and potential changes in needs, may preclude buying the large quantities that would yield the lowest cost consistent with performance and quality.

There is one other element in this cost picture. The lowest possible cost consistent with all the constraints also means that the purchasing work must get the most results for the least expenditure—or, to use an old military and aerospace term, the company needs to maximize the cost-effectiveness of the purchasing work. Management needs from purchasing are not satisfied if a huge, expensive organization pushes up the costs, even if that organization buys proficiently. Neither are they satisfied if the entire energy of the purchasing organization is used up in getting out today's purchase orders.

Now the requirements statement should read:

Buy the right things at the lowest possible cost, consistent with adequate performance and quality, *while buying in the right quantity at the right time,* and *maximizing cost-effectiveness of purchasing work.*

But we are still not finished. Company management has two more things it needs from its purchasing activity.

Management needs to know both what purchases *have* cost and what they *will* cost to be able to measure and plan the company's financial performance. The former requires a good process of reconciling purchase orders with items actually received and with invoices, plus good accounting records. The latter requires good purchase cost estimation. Because knowing what purchases will cost should precede buying decisions, let's put this requirement first.

As a last requirement, every employee has a responsibility to protect company assets. Purchasing activity carries risks of legal action by the company toward vendors, or *vice versa*, as well as action by the government for nonobservance of regulations. Purchases themselves carry the risk of theft.

What Management Needs From Its Purchasing Activity

Now we can finally make a comprehensive statement of what company management needs from its purchasing activity:

> *To know what purchases cost:* To buy the right things at the lowest possible cost, consistent with adequate performance and quality, while buying in the right quantity at the right time, and maximizing cost-effectiveness of purchasing work; *while protecting work and assets.*

Before proceeding to the satisfaction of these needs, we should discuss one more tradeoff: leasing versus buying. These are alternative ways to acquire needed items, a different kind of tradeoff. However, the subject comes up so frequently that people involved in purchasing should understand what leasing involves and when and why it makes sense.

Tradeoff: Leasing vs. Buying

You can view a lease as formalized renting, where commitment is made for a year or more. The lessee acquires the right to the use of property owned by the lessor. Although there is no legal transfer of title, many leases transfer substantially all ownership risks and rights to the lessee.

Because of the last two points, leasing is really just another choice of debt financing. As such, the lease-or-buy decision is a financial decision, the province of the chief financial officer. Office professionals should not care, unless perhaps a lease saddles them with a maintenance arrangement in which they have no confidence. Even in that case, they should argue for a lease arrangement with better maintenance, rather than arguing that the item should be bought rather than leased.

Types of Leases

There are a variety of lease forms. The main variables are the length of time versus the useful life of the item being leased, and the agreement on what happens to the property at the end of the lease. Many leases carry a provision that the lessee may buy the item at the end of the lease period, either at a stated price or a market-related price to be determined at that time. A payout lease is one in which the lessor recovers full cost and expenses. A non-payout lease is the opposite; at the end of the lease, the lessor reclaims the property and either sells or re-leases it.

From an accounting viewpoint, there are also two different forms of leases: operating and capitalized. An operating lease does not have to be entered on the balance sheet as a liability, being treated only as periodic rental expense on the profit and loss statement. A capitalized lease is one that has to be shown as a liability. This is governed by generally accepted accounting principles (GAAP) and depends on whether the lessee can acquire ownership cheaply or automatically at the end of the lease, the lease term versus the useful life of the property, and the relation of total lease payments to the value of the property. In most business situations, accountants naturally seek to structure leases as the operating variety.

Advantages and Disadvantages of Leasing

The advantages of leasing relative to financing a purchase are flexibility, usually fewer financial restrictions, and (sometimes) avoidance of having to record a liability. Regarding flexibility, often obsolescent equipment can be upgraded easier and cheaper in a leasing situation than when it is owned. Also, sometimes the tax laws confer financial advantages that cannot be obtained when buying equipment, another reason why leasing is a financial decision. Regarding financial restrictions, business loans usually carry agreements that, among other things, limit the size of other company debt. Operating leases are usually not subject to such loan restrictions.

The disadvantages of leasing are that costs are usually higher overall and that the lessee does not quite have full control over the leased item. When borrowing to buy, the lender has to make money on the loan. When leasing, the leasing company has to make money and its lenders have to make money. Thus, the lessee has to pay enough for two profits, rather than just the lender's profit. Regarding control, usually leased items cannot be modified without lessor approval, which may be important as time passes and needs change.

The Lease or Buy Decision

In addition to which alternative is cheaper, chief financial officers decide whether to lease or buy based on borrowing power available, current debt limits and restrictions, and whether they want to add a liability to the balance sheet. These are company-unique and management judgment factors, but we can generalize about the strictly financial decision.

The alternatives appear to be buying for cash, borrowing to buy, or leasing. However, buying for cash should include consideration of the cost of money—that is, the interest rate at which the company can borrow—because buying one item for cash means that the company will probably have to borrow sometime to buy other things. Money is never free; even if it is in your pocket, spending it means going without interest that you could earn on that pocketful.

Thus, the financial comparison is between borrowing to buy and leasing. A simple approximation is to determine the total amount of payments if the purchase price is borrowed for the same term as the contemplated lease and compare that to the total amount of lease payments. The smaller total is the better deal. Remember, however, to include all costs: closing costs, differences in maintenance costs, and the like.

However, the timing of payments is also important: there may be down payments, balloon payments at the end, and/or an existing borrowing may have a different term than the lease. Therefore, a rigorous analysis must introduce the concept of the time value of money.

The basic idea is that a dollar in possession today is worth more than a dollar received in the future, because interest can be earned on today's dollar. That is, if you have $100.00 today and can invest it safely at 5 percent interest, you will have $105.00 in one year. In the second year, the $105.00 earns 5 percent, so $110.25 is in hand at the end of the second year. If someone offers you a choice of $100.00 today or $115.00 guaranteed in two years, and you can invest at 5 percent, which should you take? Take the $115.00 With the $100.00 you will have $110.25 in two years. The present value of the $115.00 in two years is $115.00 divided by 1.05 (one plus the interest rate) to determine the one-year amount that would yield $115.00 in two years, divided by 1.05 again, or $104.31, the present amount that would yield $115.00 in two years at 5 percent.

The concept allows comparison of streams of cash that are unequal in both time and amount by pulling both streams back to the equivalent present value. Thus down payments, balloon payments, different terms, and such can all be included in one rigorous analysis. Such analysis is called *discounted cash flow analysis*, and the result of analyzing such a stream of cash is called the *net present value*. Calculation is cumbersome for complex cash streams, but financial calculators and computer spreadsheet programs do it quickly and easily.

For smaller companies, the ease of upgrading plus the automatic nature of the maintenance decision sometimes leads them to lease technical equipment, such as computers, somewhat independently of the financial considerations. However, that does not change the fact that the lease-or-buy decision is fundamentally financial.

8

Specifying, Estimating, and Protecting

Visualize purchasing as a building. Obtaining the lowest costs consistent with constraints is the foundation, but an entire structure is required above that foundation to achieve effective purchasing: knowing what purchases cost, buying items with the right performance and quality, and protecting work and assets. Satisfying the foundation needs is the subject of chapter 9. This chapter covers activities that promote satisfaction of the structural needs:

- Specifying needed items so purchases match performance and quality needs.
- Estimating future purchase costs so management can plan and anticipate the company's financial performance.
- Protecting against legal action and theft, so the company's assets are not suddenly depleted.

How to Specify Needed Items

A *specification* is the statement of the characteristics or requirements of a product, process, or service. Particularly when the specifier is not the buyer, the right items cannot be bought without good specifications.

Office professionals who specify purchases should keep in mind that specifications have two functions: (1) communicating to a vendor what the specifier wants, and (2) providing criteria against which the supplied goods and services are evaluated. Except for a few simple things like consulting contracts, oral understandings between customer and vendor are never enough. Except in the smallest companies, remember that acceptability of purchased items will first be evaluated by people other than the specifier. Proper specifications, chosen from the types described here and made as simple as possible without losing effectiveness, are a key to satisfactory purchases.

Various ways of specifying, and combinations of those ways, are appropriate for different kinds of purchases:

Brand names

Physical or chemical characteristics

Samples

Engineering drawings

Standards

Good commercial practice

Performance

Specification by brand name ("a Lincoln car") is the simplest, even if it has to include a manufacturer's model ("a Lincoln Continental car"), catalog, or part number ("an IXYS Company IXGM40N60A transistor"). Such a specification, however, limits the purchasing function in obtaining lower costs or other suppliers. A useful modification is "[specific brand name] or equivalent," which can be sufficiently descriptive while giving purchasing some negotiating latitude.

Specification by physical or chemical characteristics (.75- × .025-inch heavy duty steel strapping") is useful for a variety of items and lends itself to evaluation by the company or independent laboratories.

Providing a sample is useful and sometimes the only way to specify things such as cloth, artwork, and printing.

Engineering drawings are universally used in manufacturing and construction to communicate configuration and requirements of machinery, instruments, construction elements, subassemblies, etc. Unless they can be bought with part or model numbers, no manufacturing or construction components should be bought without drawings.

Standards

Many things can be bought with standard specifications developed by industry or government. Government MIL SPECS describe an amazing variety of items that military contractors buy, and they must be followed unless waivers are obtained. At the other government extreme, local building codes expressed in specifications and standards describe construction elements that must be bought and used.

Many industries, ranging from computer software to paint, have developed standards that can be used as purchase specifications, often in conjunction with other means of description. Some are published with rigorous description; some are just recognized fact. Everyone knows normal household voltage, for example, and that the U.S. electric power industry delivers alternating current.

Some businesses set company standards for items frequently bought to ensure that everyone uses the same items. These may directly constitute purchase specifications or specify a vendor and a range of items.

In many cases, the shorthand specification of "good commercial practice" has sufficient descriptive meaning for both users and suppliers.

Performance Specifications

For large projects and customized technology, the buyer specifies the use of the item plus values of performance parameters that must be achieved, leaving the design to the vendor. This category of specification is generally used in the initial proposal process and is almost universally followed during the project by specifications for design and configuration, workmanship, performance testing, and so on. Military weapon systems, for example, are governed overall by performance specifications but may use every form discussed here as subordinate specifications.

Estimating Purchase Costs

This subject was covered in Part I as it applied to budgeting—that is, estimating purchase costs over the next year. When estimating costs for purchasing purposes, the time frame is shorter. Here the concerns are the next purchases, purchase costs associated with alternative plans and programs under consideration, and purchase costs associated with implementing new ways of doing things. The same reasoning and sources of cost information apply, but more specifics are known about needs, and there is more emphasis on the higher-quality sources.

Sources of Purchase Cost Estimates

Following are the sources of purchase cost information, in order of decreasing quality:

Published information
Firm quotations

Vendor estimates

Experience

Questioned trends

Knowledgeable advice

The Best Sources

First on the list, and simplest, are costs available from published price information: price lists, catalogs, etc. These are obviously known and reliable prices, but there is still a question of forthcoming price changes, if the purchase is not to be made immediately. Some industries and vendors publish price changes in advance, some do not. Relationships with existing vendors, telephone calls to multiple vendors, and general industry knowledge are the best available sources about forthcoming price changes.

When published prices are not available, the only fully accurate source of purchase cost estimates is firm vendor quotations. These commit the vendor to sell at a given price, usually for a given time period. Unless a current relationship or other information makes vendor selection clear, multiple vendors should always be solicited for such firm quotations, so the buyer knows the best price and an average price.

The Other Sources

In the early stages of planning before requirements are firm, or when time is short, vendor estimates (often called "budgetary quotations") are often the best information that can be obtained. However, judgment must be applied, because that estimate does not represent a binding vendor commitment. Multiple vendors should again be solicited, and knowledge used about the vendor's past estimate accuracy, the industry, price trends, etc.

There is no substitute for experience when evaluating vendor estimates and coming price changes, and cost estimating in the very early stages of planning. Experience of purchasing and operating people is also the best source for purchases of items whose prices vary frequently, such as food and commodity prices. Some kinds of these variable items can be converted to known prices by contract for a specific time period, but most food for a restaurant, for example, will vary from week to week. In such cases, experience, vendor knowledge and communication, and industry knowledge are the only available sources.

Recent trends can be used to predict prices, but only after their continuation is questioned, as discussed in Part I. Because of the different time scales, buyers use trends less than budgeters, relying more on experience, knowledge, and vendor communication.

Finally, when none of the above are available, advice from the most knowledgeable people is the only source. Again, this applies more to budgeting in the sense of "the last resort." However, using knowledgeable advice—from operating and purchasing people, from respected vendors, and from outside experts—assists the process of purchase cost estimating from all the sources discussed here.

Protecting Against Legal Action

Office professionals and other operating people should understand the potential for serious business legal problems. Anyone can sue anyone else about anything; in the United States, it often seems that many people are ready to do just that. Lawsuits can have ruinous financial consequences; even if they do not, they can still capture executive and employee time for weeks and months.

There is no way to guarantee that a company will not be sued. However, there are a number of things that companies and operating people can do to minimize legal exposure.

Knowledge of Applicable Law

Employees should know the laws and government regulations that apply to their work. The source of that knowledge should be their company's legal counsel. Law is no place for amateurs. Even if it were, we could not hope to cover specifics for different types of businesses. However, some generalities are pertinent.

The law that underlies many business transactions is the Uniform Commercial Code (UCC), applicable in all states except Louisiana. It particularly applies to purchasing, because it prescribes many aspects of buying, transporting goods, and storage; as well as deposit and collection of checks, notes, and drafts.

Government regulations loom large in purchasing and can carry large penalties for nonobservance. Environmental regulations prescribe packaging, transport, handling, and storage of certain materials. Federal safety and transportation regulations often come into play. Local and state laws in all these areas are also a factor. Government contractors subject themselves to a number of socially motivated constraints on their purchasing, possibly including requirements that a percentage must go to minority firms or depressed areas.

Many types of businesses do not rely on written contracts, including most retailers and services. Legal responsibilities in such businesses are covered by the UCC, the antitrust laws, and other federal and state statutes.

Written contracts normally come into play for expensive and complex work and products, particularly those customized in whole or in part. A *contract* is an agreement between two or more parties in which each party binds itself to do or forbear some act and each acquires a right to what the other promises. It is thus a promise or set of promises that create a legal duty of performance.

Contract Responsibilities of Operating People

For businesses that use written contracts, office professionals and other operating people (nonfinancial and nonlegal businesss employees) should rely on lawyers and contract administrators for guidance and professional implementation. However, the appropriate operating people are the ones who must ensure that the specific content is correct. The financial consequences of a bad contract can be huge, when, for example, you have to pay for something you did not want and cannot use.

When dealing with vendors either not known or not trusted, the purpose of a contract is protection. With known and trusted vendors, however, the practical purpose is understanding. Friendship and trust can disappear rapidly when parties to a contract end up in dispute because of a misunderstanding over what was promised.

Therefore, no one should object to the effort required to achieve a good, clear, and complete contract. You sometimes hear the other party say, "We don't need to spell that out in the contract, because we understand each other." Good responses to that statement are, "Then we should have no trouble writing it down," and "Yes, but we need a record in case one of us gets hit by a truck."

Never say, "That is what the contract says, but that is not what the contractor means." In other words, never rely on a customer's good nature or spoken word to void an onerous contract provision; modify that provision or get it out of the contract. Do not sign anything that you do not understand, unless advisors that you trust, such as your lawyer or company experts, understand and agree. You must think through all the performance "what ifs" and ensure that they cannot cause large financial problems.

Finally, understand that anything you do in anticipation of a contract is at risk, no matter what a vendor's employees have said. Say that an engineer, before a contract is signed with a vendor, starts buying and tooling based on that vendor's oral assurance that a critical, unique part can be delivered in one month. That engineer cannot defend his or her actions if those parts do not arrive.

On the opposite side, understand that certain actions carry the implication of a contractual commitment that can result in damages being asserted if a contract is never signed. Say that a buyer assures a vendor that a contract is imminent and asks that the vendor start work immediately because the need is so urgent. If a contract is never signed, the company will probably be ruled liable for vendor costs and damages because of the "implied contract" contained in the direction given by the buyer.

Settling Disputes

In this imperfect world, some purchases and contracts will result in disputes. The closer to the problem the dispute can be settled, the cheaper and faster the settlement will be. The worst way to settle a dispute is a lawsuit. Work hard to keep disputes out of court, because lawsuits take so long, cost so much, and there is seldom a real winner. (As is often said, the only real winners in a lawsuit are the lawyers.) In fact, only a large lawsuit is worthwhile; for smaller disputes, the legal action will cost more than the amount that can be won.

The first and best way to resolve a dispute, if possible, is direct discussion between appropriate operating and purchasing people on both sides. The next best is direct discussion between higher operating managements. The next is discussion and negotiations between lawyers. Only if all these fail, should a lawsuit be used as a last resort.

There is one more useful alternative to a lawsuit: arbitration. The parties to a dispute agree to accept the decision of a tribunal of one or more men or women of stature from business or technical fields. (A typical selection method is for each side to select one arbitrator, and those two select a third arbitrator.) In arbitration, the rules of procedure and evidence are relaxed compared to those of a court, legal costs are less, and settlements come faster. Many contracts contain clauses in which the parties agree contractually to arbitration as a dispute settlement vehicle. A common source for arbitrators is the American Arbitration Association, a public-service, not-for-profit organization with headquarters in New York and offices in all major U.S. cities.

Other Legal Protectors

Other things that companies and operating people can do to help minimize legal exposure include the following:

- Use only top-flight lawyers. They are worth every penny they cost. Never accept the lowest bid for legal services.

- Document things like purchase specifications, orders, and related decisions as objectively and precisely as possible. Such documentation may be the difference between winning and losing a dispute, particularly if the other side charges favoritism, lack of diligence, or incompetence.

- Avoid unsupported promises, threats, disclosure of confidential information, and any other loose communication. Always think about how statements or letters may sound in a deposition or courtroom.

- Regularly purge files of unneeded documents. There is almost surely an old document in some file in which someone argues against a decision that management subsequently made on some matter. Even if long since discredited, that document will be found and used (to show stupidity, bad faith, or whatever) by opposition lawyers in a variety of lawsuits that may come up.

Protection Against Theft

The potential for theft losses is a particular concern associated with purchasing, simply because of the large amounts of money and transactions involved.

Theft against companies takes a number of forms. Theft by employees of physical things—tools, personal computers, inventory items, and the like—is minimized by physical security and a system of approvals and accounting for company property taken off company premises. Money theft by employees is minimized by control procedures and financial audits of cash, material receipt and payment, and reimbursed employee expenses.

Theft by nonemployees can be from company premises, in transit, or at a noncompany location. The first is again minimized by physical security. The others are beyond company control, except to deal with competent and reputable shippers and to exercise care in leaving company property elsewhere.

The newer and increasing category of theft is by computer. As computer networks grow, there are more ways for unauthorized entry into company computers for theft of money or information or for use of company resources. Safeguarding computer systems is a major modern problem and should be attacked by professionals. Money has to be spent on hardware, software, and techniques to minimize such theft. In addition, management should be vigilant for actions by competitors that indicate possible possession of company information and should pay attention to protection of company documents and prevention of loose talk by employees.

The best attitude toward theft is unwavering intolerance, apprehension, and prosecution. The best attitude toward *potential* theft is to hope everyone is honest and treat them as if they are, but to assume that there are dishonest people in every group and to devise protective measures accordingly. While complete absence of theft can never be guaranteed, there is no excuse for just hoping for the best without realistic safeguards.

Purchasing Control Mechanisms

Management wants purchasing controlled as an aid in satisfying all its purchasing needs and to, for example, keep organizations or employees from buying things that are contrary to management direction. However, such control mechanisms are also an important element of protection against theft. Employees may attempt to buy things for their own use. Buyers may be tempted to obtain kickbacks (compensation) from vendors as a reward for placing the order. Therefore, it makes sense to discuss purchasing control mechanisms as part of protection against theft.

The best defenses against abuse of purchasing are control systems that embody these five principles:

Separation of authority for
    Specifying
    Ordering
    Receiving
    Paying
Proper approvals
Multiple approvals for large purchases
Verification procedures
Outside audits

Authority is separated, first, because the different tasks require different skills and knowledge. It is also a control technique because each stage of the process is a check on the others for mistakes or deliberate theft. The theory regarding the latter is that the probability of multiple conspirators is much lower than the probability of a single dishonest person.

Proper approvals means approvals by the people with the relevant operating, financial, and procedural responsibility. The first are the users or specifiers of the purchases. For complex operations, this involves a specified sequence of documents, such as the progression from engineering design to drawings to bills of material to material requests to purchase orders. Financial responsibility generally means budget responsibility for the items to be purchased. Procedural responsibility means assurance that proper procedures have been followed and approvals obtained, plus the authority to question material requests. This procedural responsibility is ordinarily held by purchasing managers or their superiors.

Most companies employ control systems with thresholds of dollars and types of purchases that need multiple levels of approval. For example, all capital equipment purchases as well as any purchase over $50,000 may require the approval of the division vice president. Finance organization approval, concurrence, or agreement that an item is within budget may also be required for certain purchases. The trade-off is protection versus bureaucracy; more approvals may protect company funds but make the acquisition of needed material take longer and may involve people without personal knowledge of the need.

Verification procedures are the employee, paper, and computer data sequences that match purchase request, purchase order, receipt of goods, and payment for goods. Many companies automate these procedures. This is efficient and effective, as long as intelligent humans stay in control.

Outside audits provide independent verification that the control mechanisms are working and that the purchasing process is not being abused. *Outside* means outside the specifying–ordering–receiving–paying chain, not necessarily outside the company. This purchase control sequence is a common area of emphasis for a company's internal audit function. If there is no such function, outside financial auditors investigate the area periodically. A private company with no regular financial audit can arrange periodic purchasing audits by outside accountants.

Detection of determined and creative theft cannot be guaranteed but theft is made more difficult by good control mechanisms and management attention to them. Receipt of kickbacks by buyers may be particularly difficult to detect. The main defenses are continual verification by purchasing and financial management that competitive bidding is being used, suitable vendors are being sought, and good prices and quality are being obtained. Sometimes, the first notice of a buyer seeking kickbacks comes from angry vendor salespeople, but they must have confidence in management to come forward.

9

Achieving Lowest Possible Cost

Now we come to satisfaction of the "foundation" need: achieving the lowest possible cost consistent with the structural needs plus the constraints of quantity and time. Activities that promote this satisfaction are

- Inventory management that tells a company when and how much to order
- Competitive bidding that enables the company to unearth the best available prices
- A set of techniques that maximize a company's buying power and thus improve costs and service
- Other techniques that reduce purchase costs
- Practices that maximize the effectiveness of purchasing work while minimizing its costs

Managing Inventory

Probably every company in which inventory is important manages (minimizes) it better than in the past, with mostly management rather than clerical effort. Probably every sizable company has its inventory accounting computerized.

Inventory is minimized by receiving as little as possible, as close as possible to the date it is needed. Smaller inventory reduces working capital, increasing return on investment. Putting it another way, smaller inventory allows a higher level of revenue for a given financial capacity.

The General Problem

The essence of inventory management is the tradeoff between its minimization and the increased costs and/or lost revenue that result from material shortages:

Smaller inventory yields:
  Better return on investment
  More business capacity for given financial capacity
  but possibly
  Increased costs
  Lost production and sales

Sales can be lost or production schedules missed if retail products or factory material are not on hand at the right time.

A wide selection of inventory management computer software is available, aimed at different kinds of manufacturing, distribution, and retailing. Appropriate solutions vary with number of parts and products, complexity, component versus assembly effort, processes, cost structures, and so on. The overall task can be illustrated, however, by discussing the generic retailing and distribution problem and the generic manufacturing problem.

Distribution and Retailing

Distributors and retailers generally have the situation that demand for an inventory item is unrelated to other inventory items and often use *stock replenishment systems*. Reorder points are set at given inventory levels for different items, based on associated costs and expected demand.

Such systems may use *economic order quantities (EOQ)*, the size of order than minimizes total costs by, as the math turns out, making acquisition costs equal to holding costs. The EOQ depends on unit demand and cost, acquisition costs (such as clerical, vendor selection, and incoming inspection costs), holding costs (such as interest storage, pilferage, and clerical costs), and the cost of being out of inventory (such as delayed output and sales, unproductive personnel time, and the effect of late delivery on future orders).

Manufacturing

In manufacturing, the more typical problem is an inventory of interrelated items, such as the components and subassemblies for a product.

Demand for the components depends on the demand for the products. *Material requirements planning (MRP)* translates a master production schedule into time-phased requirements for the needed material. Inputs to an MRP system are the production schedule, inventory on hand and on order, lead times, and bills of materials. The MRP system explodes each product into all its assemblies, subassemblies, and components and offsets lead times. The outputs are purchase orders, rescheduling or cancellations for production schedule changes, expediting, and management reports.

Just-in-time (JIT) purchasing aims to have material supplied to a factory exactly when it is needed, approaching the ideal situation of zero inventory. It requires close relationships among design, purchasing, and vendors, and parts must be free from defects. JIT and MRP can complement each other, but generally JIT is appropriate for the manufacture of a small range of products, with production schedules fixed for several months. MRP is more appropriate for an environment where schedules are unpredictable and products complex and is particularly useful when rescheduling is a frequent problem.

Competitive Bidding

Except for unique items available only from one vendor, competitive quotations should be obtained annually or at least every two years, for all purchased items. Even the best vendors need to be kept on their toes; if they feel certain of a customer's business, both prices and service will eventually degrade.

Some buyers and users resist this because of feelings of loyalty, sympathy, or indispensability toward particular vendors. On rare occasions, loyalty and sympathy are valid—if, for example, a vendor saves the company by working literally night and day to satisfy a requirement, or if an excellent small vendor would go bankrupt without business that is a relatively minor amount to the customer company. Most of the time, however, such feelings are misplaced and should not be allowed. Examples like the following are real and all too common:

- A shipping manager who resisted discontinuing a container vendor who charged a huge price premium, because of the "invaluable" free design help he received from that vendor. The truth is that all good container vendors supply good and free design help as a cost of obtaining and retaining business. There is no need to pay a price premium to get it. After his vice president insisted, he finally chose a new vendor and is both pleased with the great new design ideas he is getting plus the much lower prices.

- An inexperienced manager of a janitorial service who "couldn't do without" an expensive vendor who kept solving problems for her by suggesting new materials and cleaning products. When her superior insisted, she found a much cheaper vendor whose help, to her surprise, turned out to be even better.

Business managers are responsible for buying adequate performance and quality at the lowest price, not for charity and certainly not for paying a premium price just so they can be comfortable. Periodic competitive bidding helps get those lowest prices.

Choosing Candidate Vendors

The first step in the competitive bidding process is choosing vendors who will be asked to bid. Unless the company is dissatisfied with them, current vendors should obviously be included. In addition, two to four other candidate vendors should ordinarily be sought.

The following are the sources for the best vendors to put on the list:

- Personal knowledge and experience
- Knowledge and experience within the company
- Solicited recommendations from other companies
- The telephone Yellow Pages
- State and national business and industry directories
- Trade associations
- Manufacturers for authorized distributors
- State governments for licensed/approved companies

Personal or company knowledge and experience are always the best sources. Otherwise, the sources' value naturally vary with the items being bought. A factory looks locally for a janitorial service vendor, probably regionally for packing materials, but nationally or internationally for manufacturing components. The Yellow Pages will not help in the last, nor will national directories help in the first. State governments will tell you insurance companies and toxic waste handlers approved to do business within the state, but cannot help with office supplies, fork lifts, and so on.

The actual choice of candidates can usually be done by phone, generally describing requirements, determining vendors' applicability and interest, and the preliminary comfort level with them. Requirements, questions, and dissatisfactions should be discussed, getting their ideas and alternative suggestions. Candidates should be told that the procurement will be competitive and that a written request for quotation (RFQ) will be sent.

Choosing candidate vendors can be a bit superficial. Some selected candidates will decide not to bid, and there is always too much work to do and too little time. The detailed checking can wait and be limited to the vendors who submit attractive quotations.

Soliciting Candidate Vendors

To be successful, a competitive bidding process must generate responsive quotations that result in the best possible prices. To be evaluated properly, responses must be comparable in all respects. To get the best prices, bidders should be told that the procurement is competitive and the amount of potential business that the company represents. To get the best results, vendors should be asked to suggest alternative items that improve cost, quality, and/or service (in addition to quoting the exact requested items, for comparability).

Bidders should also feel that they have been treated fairly. (Some losing bidders will not, however, no matter how objective the process was. One time, I told a loser that his prices were more than 10 percent higher than the winner. In a loud voice, he said, "There is *no way* that I could be off more than 10 percent." I felt like asking him, but naturally did not, if he found calling a potential customer a liar to be a good selling technique.)

To these ends, the request for quotation (RFQ) should always be in writing, so that all vendors have the same information. It should state that the procurement is competitive and give the names of the competitors. It should contain all the specifics and detail necessary for complete and responsive quotations. At the same time, it should avoid committing the company to any course of action, using words such as "intends," "evaluate the feasibility," and "reserves the right to...".

Although the specifics and detail vary with the type of items being purchased, in general, RFQ information should include the following:

- The company name and address.
- The intent of the bidding process, such as "The company hopes to select a single bidder for all fuel oil for at least a year."

- The names of the vendors being invited to bid.
- Selection criteria, such as "To obtain the lowest overall cost without sacrificing quality or service."
- The estimated annual purchases of the expense category in question, together with a reservation that this amount is not guaranteed (unless it is), such as "The company spent $X on packing materials over the past year, and anticipates, but does not guarantee, a similar amount in the next twelve months."
- Specific items to be bid, with adequate item descriptions or specifications, typical order quantities, and estimated annual usage.
- Requests for alternative suggestions for items that will improve cost, quality, and/or service.
- The quotation due date, to whom and where to send it, and to whom to direct questions in the meantime.
- That final-price quotations are desired, stating the intent that no further price negotiations will take place after the bid responses. (This is both fair and cost-effective, removing the potential of spending time negotiating, giving some vendors more information than others, and letting the procurement process get confused.)
- The intent to meet with one or more bidders before making a final decision.

A sample RFQ for office supplies that meets these requirements follows.

[Company letterhead]

[date]

[Salesperson name]

[Vendor company]

[Vendor company address]

Dear [salesperson]

As we discussed, this is a request for quotation (RFQ) for office supplies for ABC Co. The intent is minimize cost without sacrificing quality or service by choosing one or two vendors for all office supplies for at least the next year. This RFQ is being sent to current vendors [   ], [   ], and [   ] and candidate vendors [   ],[   ], and [   ].

ABC, an industrial supplies distributor, currently buys office supplies at an annual rate of $XX,000. In addition to headquarters, delivery to the following branch locations is required: [branch locations].

Enclosed is a list of yy items, their current annual quantities, and typical order sizes, that made up about 70 percent of purchases during the past year. Please (1) quote specific prices for all items in the enclosure, or as many as you are interested in supplying; (2) indicate a general pricing structure for other items, such as a particular discount from an identified list price; and (3) indicate the length of time you guarantee various prices and/or the amount of notice of price changes that you will give.

The following points also apply to your quotation. Please:

1. Direct all questions to me at [phone number].

2. Mail or fax your response to me so that it reaches me by [date]. My mailing address is [address]. My fax number is [fax number].

3. Quote as delivered to ABC's various locations, if possible. Otherwise, include a description or schedule of delivery charges.

4. Present any suggestions you have for reducing ABC's office supplies costs, such as alternative but equivalent products (quote prices for these, as well as quoting the listed item), different usage, and different buying practices and procedures.

5. Consider this a final-price proposal. We do not intend to negotiate price further after receiving these quotations. We may wish to meet with you, however, before making a final decision.

Thank you for cooperating in our efforts to reduce ABC's office supplies costs.

[closing]

Selecting the Vendor

After receiving the RFQ responses, unless one is clearly best and the vendor is known, the buyer should pick the two or three most attractive and study them in detail. Meet with the vendors to develop comfort, and explore details of ordering and problem-solving procedures. If practical, visit their facilities, because more valid impressions will come from meeting more vendor employees and seeing how those facilities look and operate. Get customer references, particularly for small or unknown vendors, if that will help establish comfort. If the vendor is small and the purchase need is critical, insist on access to financial statements and lender references.

If applicable, set up an initial vendor test before making a final decision. This is not practical for phone service, for example, but product vendors in many industries will supply free samples. In other vendor industries, buyers can negotiate special prices for a small test order.

Do not sign a contract for purchases unless the vendor industry only operates that way or unless a contract offers clear advantages, such as attractive long-term price guarantees. Otherwise, a contract is not necessary, and only restricts the company's future choices.

Finally, select the vendor that appears to offer the best combination of price, performance, quality, and comfort. Plan to stay with that vendor for at least a year unless unsolvable problems arise.

Regarding problems, the perfect vendor does not exist; companies should expect some problems, particularly in initial transition. The best test of vendor quality is not absence of problems as much as how they react to inevitable problems. Companies should work patiently with new vendors, remembering why they were chosen in the first place. However, if the vendor does not react satisfactorily after full discussion, stop doing business with them and go back to the second choice of the RFQ process.

Maximizing Buying Power

The idea of "buying power" is that the prices of most manufactured items, printing, and some services vary inversely with the amount ordered—that is, the bigger the order, the lower the unit price. Thus, the more buying power a company can use, the lower its unit prices and therefore its overall purchase costs.

Printing is usually the premier example; because most of the cost is in the set-up and little in the production, the total cost of 5,000 forms, for example, is often only a few dollars more than 1,000. This is why the world is full of unused business cards—it seldom makes sense to buy less than 500 at a time, and then title, address, or area code change, and another order for 500 goes to the printer.

Buying power also affects service: the more a customer buys, the more important that customer is to the vendor, and the more attention that customer will get. This gives buying power a sort of relative dimension, in addition to the importance of absolute amounts. If a company is a small vendor's largest customer, that company will get its best service and attention to problems, even if it does not buy in IBM-like quantities.

Smaller companies will never have the buying power of the giants, but all can improve their costs and service by maximizing whatever inherent buying power their size commands. They do this by buying in the largest quantities consistent with (1) the price–quantity–time tradeoff relative to the cost of money for non-revenue-producing items or maximizing return on investment for revenue producing items; (2) available storage space; and (3) the potential that needs will change before the entire purchase quantity is used.

The following are some techniques for buying in the largest quantities. Not all of them work for all kinds of purchases, but all should be pursued to see if they are valid for purchases of interest and then used where they apply.

Standardizing and Limiting Items

If companies allow different operations and individuals to buy their personal preference of various supplies and services, they will buy small quantities of a large number of items and pay higher prices. This is true if different company locations each buy their own telephone service. It is also true if different locations and individuals specify their own preference in office supplies like filing systems and copy paper, or janitorial supplies like paper towels and cleaning fluids.

Let's say that six different company offices independently buy copy paper. Requirements and buying discipline vary, so sometimes one ream (500 sheets) is bought, other times five cartons (one carton equals ten reams). Paper prices vary widely over time, but let's say that the company, buying this way, now pays anywhere from $2.50 to $7.00 per ream, averaging about $3.00. If the company chose one type of copy paper and bought ten cartons at a time to supply all its offices, a price of $2.35 per ream would be reasonable, about 22 percent below its current average price.

Similarly, standardizing and limiting the features of six different long-distance telephone services into one company-wide service from one vendor could save 20 to 30 percent. The same thing applies to everything from manufacturing components to toilet paper. Automobile manufacturers, for example, put major effort into using the same parts and assemblies in most of their different models.

A collateral benefit is often cutting overall usage and thus saving more money. Standardizing and limiting focus enough attention on the cost category that people start looking harder at how much they really need. The person who has a storeroom full of varied, little-used supplies will tend to use them before buying more and not order such amounts and varieties again.

Using Only One or Two Vendors

Buying everything of a type from one vendor is a direct extension of standardizing and limiting items, with the added dimension of making the company a more important customer of that single vendor. In the example of standardizing copy paper, an even lower price could be obtained if all company copy paper is bought from the same vendor. Further, if the amount is large enough, that vendor will think twice before passing along the next paper price increase.

For reasons of quality and continuing dependability, companies may choose to buy critical items from two sources. They must understand, however, that this practice will probably increase their prices. In any event, spreading business beyond two vendors, or beyond one for noncritical items, just weakens buying power. It also increases buying and clerical costs because multiple vendors and orders make more work for employees.

Using Blanket Orders

For many manufacturing components and commodities, so-called blanket orders are a way to get large-quantity prices without increasing outward cash flow or storage requirements. A blanket order is a commitment to buy a given amount over a lengthy time period (often a year for manufacturing components, sometimes longer for commodities), while taking delivery and paying for purchases across the period as needed. The vendor is agreeing to a price, to store items, and to periodic payment in return for a quantity commitment by the customer.

The customer must be confident that the entire quantity will be needed and that its specifications will not change, because it must buy the committed quantity. Nothing wastes money faster than buying things that cannot be used.

Further, not all vendor industries offer blanket orders, which work best for widely used, off-the-shelf kinds of items. For things made to order, or custom made, vendors usually will not offer blanket orders unless the customer will pay a storage charge and probably a price increase that reflects the vendor's cost of money for its production now tied up in inventory.

For types of purchases for which they are offered and within the constraint of confidence in ultimate use, however, blanket orders are excellent cost cutters. In looking for unfamiliar items, buyers should always inquire whether vendors offer them.

Taking Advantage of Price Breaks

In some vendor industries, the unit price decreases with every substantial increase in order quantity. Printing is again an extreme example. However, some purchased items carry discrete "price breaks" instead. A manufacturing part, for example, may have a minimum order quantity of 100 pieces, one unit price for 100 to 5,000 pieces, another unit price for 5,001 to 20,000 pieces, and so on. Again, when looking for unfamiliar items, buyers should always inquire about price breaks, and take advantage of them where possible.

For a particular electronic part, for example, a company may anticipate needing 9,000 pieces for the year, which are available on a blanket order. The buyer learns, however, that there is a price break at 10,000 pieces. If the break is large enough that 10,000 pieces cost less than 9,000, it is clearly better to buy 10,000 instead. If the price is the same, one should still buy 10,000, because the last 1,000 are free, and, who knows, better business might generate a need for additional parts. If 10,000 cost "a little more" than 9,000, the decision involves more judgment, but buying 10,000 may still make sense. If reasonably confident that the part will still be used next year, the 10,000 should still be bought. However, if even the need for 9,000 seems optimistic, or if business appears to be turning down, stay with the 9,000, or even less.

Other Ways of Cutting Purchasing Costs

Minimizing purchase costs within all the constraints is ultimately a matter of being hard-nosed with vendors and stingy with the company's money. No vendor is obligated to give customers its lowest possible prices; it is up to buyers to probe energetically for the lowest price at which vendors are willing to sell. Competitive bidding is one way to do this, but there are a number of ways to be hard-nosed and stingy about purchases. Four such ways to reduce purchase costs are the following.

Declaring Price Freezes or Cuts

The company sends a letter to *all* suppliers stating that times are tough, and that no price increases will be accepted for twelve months. The tone should not be dictatorial; rather, that vendor cooperation is needed for the company's prosperity, and therefore continued status as a good customer. A good additional paragraph is that any price increase will trigger a competitive bid. The letter should be signed by the president or a vice president so that it is viewed as serious.

Some vendors will freeze their prices, and the company has saved money. Others will ignore the letter, but continued pressure will cause some of those to give in. Buyers can say, "Didn't you get the president's letter? What are you trying to do, get me fired?" Naturally, the company must carry out the threat of competitive bidding, or such a letter will never be taken seriously again.

A more extreme version of the same process is to have the letter declare an across-the-board price reduction of a few percent instead of a freeze. This will be harder to sell, but you may be surprised at how much money is saved.

Finding Out What Other Companies Pay

Find out what other comparable companies pay for the same purchases and take that information to your vendor. Either ask for the same deal or just share the data. If the vendor has been claiming that you are getting the best price, embarrassment will probably result in an immediate price cut.

For common purchases like commodity chemicals, packing materials, office supplies, and telephone service, buyers can usually get such information from buyers at comparably-sized companies who are not competitors. For company-specific, revenue-producing items, competitors may be the only source, and the information will be harder to get. Every industry has a grapevine, and every sharp company cultivates industry information sources; sometimes you can get the information from these. However, even if you have to limit the technique to common items, with information from noncompetitors, some decent savings can result.

Cutting the Use of Purchased Goods and Services

Every company buys more than it needs of *some* kind of goods or services. Some of these are just habits, like excessive use of overnight mail. Some are viewed as rights, such as getting a new desktop computer every two years.

Aggressive control can usually save money in almost any purchase category you can name. Computer hardware and software can usually be reduced or delayed with little impact. New furniture is often bought when suitable desks, chairs, and bookcases already sit in the warehouse or empty offices. Does the company really need all the copiers that it has? Does everyone really need telephones with all the buttons and features? Are all the consultants really needed, or are some used because an outside judgment impresses the president or the board of directors? Does the company really need maintenance contracts for all the equipment presently covered? Some of them possibly never break down; paying just for repairs, and perhaps less frequent preventive maintenance, will be cheaper.

Aggressive control requires a management champion and continuing management attention. However, office professionals can lobby for such attention (and usually earn the respect and gratitude of management) and strongly influence the control.

Using an Outside Consultant

Experienced consultants can often help instill all the practices that make purchasing more effective and efficient, especially if they offer some advantages over employees in reducing purchase costs without sacrificing quality or service. First, they can be focused on cost reductions in assigned areas, whereas employees usually have more work than they can accomplish, including every day's buying. Second, good consultants have a broader knowledge of vendors and purchasing practices than most employees. Third, they offer a fresh viewpoint, free from the biases that naturally grow about current vendors; they have neither the comfort nor inertia that too often results in staying with vendors who charge excessive prices.

Beyond these things, the fact that an outside consultant has been retained sends a strong signal to current vendors that the company is serious about reducing purchase costs. Surprisingly often, professionally conducted phone calls to current vendors by such a consultant result in immediate price reductions. Comparable employee calls get the same result much less frequently, apparently because the cost cutting message is not as strong. (However, calls from a new vice president, saying that costs are just too high and soliciting vendor suggestions for lowering them, can also be quite fruitful.)

Maximizing Purchasing Cost-Effectiveness

For the most effective purchasing, the purchasing work itself must have maximum effectiveness at minimum cost. Both sides of the picture are important. The benefit of obtaining lower prices is diminished if the effort to get them is extremely expensive. On the other hand, if every bit of energy is required to accomplish today's ordering requirements, the purchasing organization can never position itself to improve effectiveness on future purchases.

First, Satisfy the Management Needs

Fortunately, everything that acts to satisfy all the other management purchasing needs also contributes to the cost-effectiveness of the purchasing work, making this somewhat a summary of our whole discussion of purchasing:

- Good specifications result in buying the right items the first time, make the requirements clear to the vendors, and make acceptance or rejection easier.
- Good cost estimation minimizes cost surprises that cause plans and requirements to change and buying to be redone.
- Protecting work and assets not only saves money from losses and lawsuits but minimizes the time and effort spent chasing after problems.
- Computerized inventory management indicates the right purchase quantities and timing, and does so with minimum purchasing effort.
- Competitive bidding both maximizes the chance of getting the lowest price and, when it results in a single vendor for a whole category of well-specified items, minimizes future buying effort.
- Standardizing and limiting items, using only one or two vendors, and using blanket orders where available not only reduce purchase prices but, again, minimize future buying effort.

For some of these practices, an old adage comes to mind: "There is never time to do it right, but always time to do it over." Competitive bidding requires some work, as does standardizing and limiting items, for example. However, once that initial work is done, future buying is not only more effective; it is easier, taking less effort and time, and thus cost. That effort and time can then be devoted continued future improvements in both effectiveness and efficiency.

Buying Like a Business

One other promoter of purchasing cost-effectiveness merits mention as a final element of effective purchasing for small companies: they should "buy like businesses, not like consumer 'shoppers'." This may seem obvious, but many small companies behave like consumers when they buy.

How do consumer "shoppers" buy? Every time they want or need something, they read ads and solicit advice from neighbors and friends. They call or visit multiple stores. In short, they energetically compare today's price, quality, and features, and make their decisions accordingly. If they are good shoppers, they get the best deals, and these are good tactics for infrequent purchases.

However, the same things are appalling wastes of resources for businesses. They may get the best deal today, but will use up the whole day doing it, and will have to repeat the same process tomorrow for other purchases. Much better "business buying" is to select one or two vendors for each major category every year, and then buy everything from such selected vendors, using all the techniques and processes that have been discussed.

The reduced daily costs and efforts of buying each item more than make up for any missed one-time bargains, and buyers have time to find better prices, quality, and service for the future.

Part III

Fruitful Financial Statement Analysis

10

Defining the Problem

The financial statements of interest are the cash flow statement, the balance sheet, and the profit and loss (P&L) statement. They are defined by these three basic accounting equations:

- Cash Flow Statement: Cash flow = Receipts − Disbursements
- Balance Sheet: Assets = Liabilities + Equity
- Profit & Loss Statement: Profit = Revenue − Expense

In addition to numerical presentations, *notes to the financial statements* always accompany them. The notes explain the numbers, are an integral part of the statements, and are important in the analysis of the numbers.

Analysis of financial statements is a major subject, a starting point for the work of acquirers, investors, lenders, securities analysts, business executives, and accountants. Many books and articles have been written about the subject, including development of many sophisticated algorithms and ratios to measure all aspects of financial performance.

Narrowing a Major Subject

Now office professionals are not expected to acquire businesses or make other major investment decisions for their companies. They have a work interest, however, in evaluating the financial condition and performance of their own companies, competitors, and vendors.

- They should want to evaluate their own companies to be able to make better business and personal decisions. As an extreme example, if company equity has been negative for some time, they should probably look for another job, no matter what their bosses tell them.

- They may have a need to evaluate competitors. Generally, healthy companies make more formidable competitors. On the other hand, competitors in financial trouble sometimes do destructive things to an industry. A company operating in bankruptcy, for example, may lower prices aggressively, hurting profits of its entire industry. (While in bankruptcy, it does not have to make principal or interest payments on its debt, and thus has a short-term financial advantage over competitors.)

- They often have to evaluate vendors. The best purchased component in the world will not help your product if the vendor cannot deliver it because of financial problems that affect its operations.

The concern about such companies is not whether they are the best investments; it is whether they will continue to operate successfully. Will they continue to be dependable, aggressive, growing, and/or whatever characteristics apply to them now? Fundamentally, then, this working concern of office professionals is whether their own company, competitors, and vendors will *survive* in a condition that will avoid reducing products and services, layoffs, and restructurings. Financial statements are the first, and possibly the only, means for them to do such survival evaluations.

Conditions of Business Survival

The obvious first conditions of business survival are profitability and cash flow. To continue to exist, a company must earn profits; it cannot spend more than it takes in over time.

However, even profitable companies with positive cash flow will not survive if they cannot meet their financial obligations: pay their debts, employees, and day-to-day bills. Occasionally we see Wall Street darlings—profitable, rapidly growing companies—suddenly fail and shut their doors. As revenue and profit grow, assets and liabilities—inventory, receivables, fixed assets, and therefore usually debt—grow rapidly as well. Any pause in revenue growth results in cash and borrowing capacity suddenly being inadequate to service these swollen balance sheet accounts. Such companies "grow themselves into bankruptcy," examples of successful companies who cannot meet their financial obligations.

This ability to meet obligations involves not only long-term debt; it also requires liquidity, or the ability to meet short-term obligations. If a profitable company has no borrowing power and cannot collect its accounts receivable fast enough to buy more materials or pay its employees, it cannot continue operations and will not survive even if it has little long-term debt.

Thus, office professionals should analyze financial statements primarily for *profitability, cash flow, and the ability to meet both long- and short-term financial obligations.* All three financial statements, plus associated information, supply indicators of the ability to meet financial obligations, while we analyze profitability and cash flow primarily in their respective statements.

Sources of Financial Statements

The Securities and Exchange Commission (SEC) requires all American public companies to publish annual and quarterly financial reports, including financial statements. These reports are mailed to all stockholders, and anyone can generally obtain them free of charge from the company. (Address the request to the corporate secretary or the manager of investor relations.) Unfortunately, privately owned companies are not required to publish reports and usually consider their financial statements confidential. Small vendors, particularly, are usually privately owned.

Further, when private companies supply financial statements, they are often *compiled*, rather than *audited*, by independent accountants. The distinction is important: *compiled* means that the accountant took management's word for all the statement inputs; *audited* means that the accountant checked and tested the inputs, so the statements constitute an independent, professional evaluation of the company. Compiled statements may give you some gross comfort or concerns, but are hardly worth analyzing; insist on audited statements if the analysis is important.

The Auditor's Letter

The *report of independent public accountants* (the "auditor's letter") always accompanies financial statements. For private companies, it is where one learns whether the statements were audited or only compiled.

For audited statements, it uses standard terminology to report results of the audit. Normally, it includes a statement like, "The financial statements present fairly, in all material respects, the financial position of [company] for [latest two years] and the results of their operations and cash flows for each of the latest three years, in conformity with generally accepted accounting principles."

The auditor's letter contains the most information if it includes another statement; that is, if it is a *qualified* report. A qualified report expresses a concern about the continued survival of the company, based on a reality (such as negative equity or a recent loss of financing) or contingency (such as a large lawsuit against the company) in its financial condition. A qualified auditor's letter should be taken very seriously, and the company watched closely. It may not be around, at least in its present form, in a year or two.

Reading this auditor's letter is thus the very first step in analyzing financial statements, done before studying the statements themselves.

Public Company Annual Reports

For public companies, the annual reports to stockholders contain the financial statements plus other information that should figure into analysis of the company:

1. *The chief executive officer's (CEO's) letter to stockholders* gives the CEO's personal comments on company financial health, past results, and future prospects.

2. *Descriptive material* is included about the company's business, products, and customers. This should be evaluated like any public relations material.

3. *Management's discussion of financial conditions and operations* explains the results reflected in the financial statements. Particularly useful is the discussion of *liquidity*, which gives information about borrowing power, dividends, how much of needed cash was generated from operations, and discussion of the expected adequacy of financial resources.

4. *Other descriptive information* includes a five- or ten-year record of things like sales, profit, and equity, perhaps with graphs and charts. Administrative information, such as names of officers and directors, company address, and annual meeting date, is also included.

The Form 10-K

Any serious financial analysis should include study of the Securities and Exchange Commission (SEC) *form 10-K* as well as the glossy annual report to stockholders. The 10-K is required annually from every public company. It is not usually distributed, but anyone can obtain it from the SEC or from the company. It differs from the annual report to stockholders in the formatted information it contains, and in its avoidance of puffery and promotion. While the annual report may extol wonderful products, the 10-K may contain scary statements like "In the event that such cash flow and financing are not sufficient for continuing operations, there is no assurance that any other source of funds will be available to the company."

Information that can be found in the 10-K, but not usually in the glossy annual report, includes the following:

- Percentage of total sales to the U.S. government
- Identification of each customer that accounted for over 10 percent of total revenue
- Dependence on critical suppliers
- The degree of competition for various products
- Obligations under significant agreements and contracts
- Financial and contractual status of real estate
- Legal proceedings, including lawyers' opinions on the likelihood that the company will prevail; and/or estimates of settlements, verdicts, or liabilities

For public companies, read the form 10-K for survival threats lurking in legal proceedings and obligations under significant agreements and contracts. Other disquieting information that could represent survival threats at some point includes high dependence on critical suppliers and a single customer accounting for the majority of revenues.

Limitations

Unfortunately, there are a number of limitations on the usefulness of financial statements and reports for analysis. The first was already mentioned: the subject applies mainly to public companies; when private companies supply financial statements, they are often compiled rather than audited. Also, financial statements are usually not published for wholly owned subsidiaries of public companies.

The second limitation is that, strictly speaking, the analysis to be described applies only to American companies. Large companies in the major industrial countries publish reliable financial statements, but the analyst must understand that standards and practices differ from country to country. For example, Japanese companies routinely have interlocking ownership, debt levels, and collection times that would raise questions in American companies.

Third, firm conclusions about a company cannot be drawn just from sets of numbers; the underlying reasons for values and ratios must be sought. The proper analytical function of financial statement numbers is to serve as indicators of possible problems and questions that should be asked. For example, a large increase in accounts receivable (sales for which payment has not yet been collected) may mean collection problems and the potential of bad debt write-offs that wipe out profits. On the other hand, it may be the result of a marketing decision to offer extended terms, made to increase eventual sales while knowingly increasing the necessary working capital (current assets minus current liabilities, or resources available to fund current operations).

Fourth, profit can often be managed, at least in the short term, and companies vary in their degree of accounting conservatism. Also, accounting rules are logical and work well on the average, but may not reflect reality in a given situation. For example, securities and real estate investments are normally valued at the lower of cost or market value. In boom times, the value of company-owned real estate may thus be considerably understated on the balance sheet.

Fifth, there are no ideal values or ratios of financial statement accounts that are best for all companies. Problem values and ratios can be determined only in the context of the company's industry and variation over time. For example, distributors' profit margins (profit divided by revenue) are almost always lower than successful manufacturers; however, they may be even more attractive because their required investment is also lower, so return on investment may be better. Thus, to be meaningful, analysis must look for comparison with the past, with competitors, and with industry averages.

Keep these limitations in mind while subsequent chapters discuss the inferences that *can* be drawn from published financial reports and statements of American public companies and the audited financial statements of private companies, when the latter can be obtained.

Fundamental Accounting Concepts

Before explaining and analyzing any of the statements, we should note that accounting is the financial language of business. It is the system or science of keeping, analyzing, and explaining the amounts of money involved in business transactions. Its purpose is to portray, in consistent and conventional ways that can be widely understood, the financial health and success of a business, as well as to maintain at all times the status of its property and obligations.

Understanding financial statements requires familiarity with two fundamental accounting concepts.

Generally Accepted Accounting Principles (GAAP)

In the United States, GAAP are the set of rules by and for the accounting profession that govern accounting practice and financial statement preparation. Following are the most important principles of the GAAP:

- Conservatism: portraying a company's financial picture in the least favorable light, whenever possible.
- Matching: pairing in time any receipts with the costs incurred in generating them.
- Realization: including on the P&L statement only those revenues that have been earned; that is, those in which a sales transaction has been completed or a service performed.
- Consolidation: including all company business and transactions during the period covered.
- Consistency: using the same method of accounting throughout all company statements and over time, unless a change is prominently announced.

The GAAP are flexible, and a number of methods of accounting are acceptable as long as consistency is maintained.

Accrual Accounting

Accrual accounting is used by most businesses, including all public companies. *Cash accounting* is similar to what you do with your personal checkbook; it records revenue, expense, and changes in balance sheet account when cash is received or paid. *Accrual accounting*, in contrast, records revenue when earned and costs, generally, when a commitment to spend is made. Also, costs paid once a year can be "spread" or accrued in equal amounts each month or quarter.

Accrual accounting follows the GAAP principle of matching, in time, revenue with all expense required to generate it. It gives a more realistic picture of financial health and success by this matching and by focusing on commitments and spreading large, infrequent costs. For example, if you use a machine every day to produce products, you get a more realistic picture of product cost by charging a bit of the machine cost to each product, as opposed to "expensing" the total machine cost the day it was bought.

11

Cash Flow

As a business begins, its owner's main financial concern is cash—how much the company has, how much it needs, how much it will get over a given time period. Cash flow for a period of time is the amount of increase or decrease in a company's cash during that period. "Cash" includes monetary instruments like checks, as well as currency.

$$\text{Cash flow} = \text{Receipts} - \text{Disbursements}$$

Receipts are simply cash taken in, while *disbursements* are cash paid out. They are never manipulated in a timing sense, making cash flow the simplest and most absolute concept in accounting. Accountants can use GAAP flexibility to record revenue, expense, and balance sheet items earlier or later and thus "manage" profit in the short term. However, the only thing accountants can do with cash is to keep score.

Cash flow remains important for any business of any size, because cash is the ultimate survival measure. If sufficient cash is neither on hand nor available from lenders, a business cannot operate, no matter what the balance sheet or the profit and loss (P&L) statement say. However, cash flow is not the best financial measure of a business. Negative cash flow is not necessarily bad; it can be good if it results from buying new factory equipment that will yield increased sales and profit. Similarly, positive cash flow is not necessarily good; it may mean that the company is not investing enough in the future, or perhaps it has received advanced payment for products that it cannot deliver.

The other two statements, the balance sheet and the P&L, are better measures of business financial health and success.

113

Explaining the Cash Flow Statement

For illustrative purposes we invent a typical cash flow statement, as we will also do for the balance sheet and profit and loss statement. We will use the fictitious ABC Corp. Different companies will have other entries, but those that we use will be found in most company's financial statements. Round numbers are used, presented always in thousands of dollars. As usual in accounting, plain numbers are positive, while numbers in parentheses are negative.

The cash flow statement is a succession of additions and subtractions in different categories that computes the "net change in cash and cash equivalents" during the year. *Cash equivalents* is a common accounting term for money market funds and the like that can be converted to cash quickly at known value; in our usage in this book, "cash" always includes such equivalents.

The following is the ABC Corp. Statement of Cash Flows.

ABC Corp. Statement of Cash Flows

Cash Flow from Operating Activities	
Net Income (Loss)	$1,800
Adjustments of net income to net cash	
Noncash expense and profit items	800
Changes in current assets and liabilities	(1,000)
Total cash flow from operating activities	1,600
Cash Flow from Investing Activities	
Capital expenditures	(1,000)
Proceeds from sale of assets	200
Investments	(100)
Total cash flow from investing activities	(900)
Cash Flow from Financing Activities	
Short-term borrowings (repayments)	(900)
Long-term borrowings (repayments)	1,000
Cash dividends paid	(600)
Total cash flow from financing activities	(500)
Net change in cash and cash equivalents	200
Cash and cash equivalents on January 1	300
Cash and cash equivalents on December 31	$500

Company balance sheets and P&L statements are always shown in essentially the same form, but you may see cash flow statements in at least two different forms. This one groups cash flows into different kinds of activities: the cash generated or used by the basic operations of the business, the amount of cash invested by and in the business (one hopes that this number is negative, a cash outflow), and the amount of financing obtained or paid off. It thus shows at a glance the effects of these different financial aspects of the business.

The other common form is "Sources and Uses of Funds," which groups items according to whether they bring cash in (sources) or pay it out (uses). Examples of sources are profit, sale of any asset, selling stock, and borrowing money. Uses include losses, costs of all kinds, and dividends paid on company stock.

Cash flow from operating activities is not just net income or profit. First, noncash expenses or profits have to be removed (added or subtracted, as appropriate) from that net income. An example of a noncash expense is depreciation, necessary to reflect aging of equipment but involving no cash expenditure. A noncash profit could occur, for example, when large price increases cause a company to revalue its inventory higher; what it owns is worth more but, again, no cash changed hands.

Second, changes in current assets and liabilities (such as accounts receivable, inventory, and accounts payable) change cash and must be reflected. That is, if inventory increased during the period, cash was spent (reduced) that does not appear in net income.

Most of the cash flow from investing activities is usually capital expenditures or purchases of equipment and facilities needed by the business. Sometimes assets are sold, and this category also reflects things like investments in other companies and investment of temporarily excess cash.

Cash flow from financing activities shows the results of borrowings and repayments of debt and things like payment of dividends on the company's stock.

After computing the net change of cash and cash equivalents, the statement ends with a connection to the balance sheet, showing cash at the beginning and end of the year.

Analyzing the Cash Flow Statement

The *net change in cash* should be positive, at least when summed over a few years. Large investments may turn one year negative, but continuing negative cash flow is a problem unless the company is a regulated, monopoly kind of utility. Such a company must continue to invest, but can be confident of getting a return on that investment.

A useful ratio is the *cash debt coverage* ratio: cash flow from operations minus dividends divided by total debt (obtained from the balance sheet). The reciprocal of this ratio (that is, one divided by the ratio) is the number of years of current cash flow needed to pay off all debt. A high ratio gives comfort that the level of debt is not too much of a burden to the current business.

Similarly, the *cash dividend coverage ratio* (cash flow from operations divided by dividends) shows the ability to pay dividends out of operating cash flow. You want this ratio to be greater than one; a healthy company does not have to borrow money to pay dividends—if a company does, you wonder why it does not decrease the dividend.

From the three main sections of the cash flow statement:

- The *ratio of cash flow from investing activities to cash flows from both operating and financing activities* compares the funds needed to the available financial resources. That is, it shows whether cash both generated internally and available externally are sufficient to fund the needed investments.

- The *ratio of cash flow from investing activities to cash flow from financing activities* shows whether external funding sources are adequate to meet investing needs.

In summary, the net change in cash provides a direct survival indicator: is the company taking in more cash than it is spending, particularly when summed over a few years? The four ratio indicators then provide considerable information about the company's ability to meet its financial obligations.

12

The Balance Sheet

If you start a manufacturing business with $50,000 cash and spend $5,000 on a machine and $5,000 on materials, your cash flow is a negative $10,000. However, the value of your business is still $50,000; you have merely exchanged $10,000 of your cash for $10,000 worth of equipment and materials. You could even argue (nonfinancially) that your business is worth more, because you now have things that will be used to make money.

The financial statement that portrays financial health is the balance sheet, based on this equation:

$$\text{Assets} = \text{Liabilities} + \text{Equity}$$

Assets are those things of value that a company owns. *Liabilities* are things of value that a company owes to someone. *Equity* is then what the company is worth, the owners' investment in the business. The terms *net worth* and *stockholders equity* are generally used interchangeably for equity, although, strictly speaking, the former applies to a proprietorship while the latter applies to a corporation. *Book value* is also a synonym for equity.

Rearranging the balance sheet equation,

$$\text{Equity} = \text{Assets} - \text{Liabilities}$$

or, in plain English, what you have equals what you own minus what you owe.

In other words, the balance sheet continuously tracks all company transactions to give a picture of what the company is worth at any particular time. The balance sheet describes a company on a particular date, typically the end of a year or quarter, while cash flow and the

117

proft and loss (P&L) statement record what has happened over a period
of time, usually a year or a quarter.

Keep in mind that the equity of a company is its accounting value
based on results of all past transactions. *Market value*, what people are
willing to pay for a company or its shares at a given time, is a completely different concept. Market value may be more or less than equity
on any particular day, depending upon what potential investors believe
the company's prospects to be.

Explaining the Balance Sheet

The balance sheet sums assets, liabilities, and equity separately; and
total assets must always equal total liabilities plus equity, as the accounting equation dictates. The following is the fictitious ABC Corp.
balance sheet:

ABC Corp. Balance Sheet

Assets

Current Assets	
Cash and cash equivalents	$500
Accounts receivable	8,000
Inventory	6,000
Prepaid expenses	500
Total current assets	$15,000
Fixed Assets	
Property, plant, and equipment	8,700
Less: accumulated depreciation	(5,000)
Intangible assets	300
Total fixed assets	$4,000
Total Assets	$19,000

Liabilities and Equity

Current Liabilities	
Short-term debt	2,000
Accounts payable	2,500

Accrued expenses	1,000
Deferred revenue	1,000
Total current liabilities	$6,500
Long-Term Liabilities	
Long-term debt	3,000
Capital lease obligations	1,500
Total long-term liabilities	$4,500
Total Liabilities	$11,000
Equity	
Preferred stock	100
Common stock	200
Additional paid-in capital	2,200
Retained earnings	5,500
Total equity	$8,000
Total Liabilities and Equity	$19,000

Assets are conventionally divided into *current assets* (cash and those things convertible into cash in the short term) and *fixed assets* (nonmonetary things like machinery and real estate that have long-term value). Liabilities are divided into *current liabilities* (obligations that must be discharged within a year) and *long-term liabilities* (those that must be discharged in more than a year). *Working capital* is a term used for current assets minus current liabilities, a measure of the company's ability to fund short-term operations.

Typical assets are *cash, accounts receivable* (money owed to the company for products and services already delivered), *inventory* (the company's stock of materials and products that eventually will be sold), *equipment*, and *land and buildings owned. Prepaid expenses* are also assets, because they have value—the right to the use of something in the future. For example, if rent were paid for a year in advance, the payment would ordinarily be recorded as an asset that decreases (is "expensed") by one-twelfth every month. *Intangible assets* are things like patents, goodwill, and capitalized computer software whose value is intellectual rather than physical.

The fixed assets of property, plant, and equipment are shown at their full value (ordinarily their cost); and *accumulated depreciation* is shown on a separate line. All such fixed assets are *depreciated* over their useful lives, and the correct fraction of their cost is *amortized*, or spread and expensed, every month. Accumulated depreciation is the total depreciation to date of the property, plant, and equipment on the balance sheet. Assume that machinery costing $600,000 is bought, judged to have a five-year useful life, and that straight-line depreciation is used. Because there are sixty months in five years, the monthly depreciation expense on the P&L statement would be one-sixtieth of the $600,000 cost, or $10,000, and accumulated depreciation on the balance sheet after three years would be 36 months times $10,000, or $360,000.

Typical liabilities are *accounts payable* (money that the company owes for things already bought and received), *debts* of all kinds, and *deferred revenue* (receipts in advance for products and services to be delivered). The latter is a liability because it is an obligation to supply products or services in the future.

Other familiar liabilities are *accrued expenses* of various kinds. If the balance sheet date is in the middle of a payroll period, for example, the payroll expenses from last payday through the statement date are accrued—that is, charged to the P&L statement as an expense and listed as a liability on the balance sheet. On the next payday that accrual is reversed, reducing accrued expenses and reducing cash.

In the *equity* section, by accounting convention, preferred and common stock are entered at an arbitrary par value, and additional amounts received for stock are entered as *paid-in capital. Retained earnings* equals the sum of all past net income minus dividends paid—that is, the total amount of net income retained over time for use by the business.

Analyzing the Balance Sheet

Because the balance sheet portrays the financial health of a business, it is the primary statement for analysis of the ability to meet financial obligations.

In analyzing the balance sheet, look first at *equity*. If equity is negative, the company is technically bankrupt and living on borrowed time. Don't select it for any long-term relationships.

If *retained earnings* are negative, either the total of all the past operations is a loss or the company has paid out more in dividends that it has earned. Both are undesirable.

Look for the amount of *intangible assets* within the fixed assets. The collateral or liquidation value of intangible assets is often questionable. If they are relatively large, compute *tangible equity* (equity minus intangible assets) and use that in evaluation, rather than equity.

A high *ratio of debt to capital* (equity plus long-term debt) is risky, a direct measure of the ability to meet financial obligations. Keep in mind, however, that there are no absolutely correct ratios, and *high* must be interpreted in terms of the company's industry, history, and perhaps some current special conditions. The notes to the financial statements give information on *debt maturities*, which are also important in determining the company's ability to pay its debts—the longer, the better—if the ratio of debt to capital is high. *Lease obligations*, also stated in the notes if material (that is, large enough to be important), are also important because they represent an obligation just like debt.

Interest rates on the debt, also found in the notes, are an independent indicator of the financial community's judgment about the company's financial health. Companies considered risky can borrow only at a few points above the prime rate. Indicators of *borrowing power* are the debt-to-capital ratio and statements in the notes about the extent of unused credit facilities.

The best kind of liability is *deferred revenue*, meaning goods or services for which customers have paid in advance. If the company has a record of successful operations, large deferred revenue is an indicator both of future profits and lack of collection problems.

Liquidity Measures

Liquidity is the ability to pay current and short-term obligations, an important element of financial health. Even if profitability, cash flow, and the ability to meet long-term financial obligations are good, adverse short-term surprises could bring operations to a halt if there is insufficient liquidity. Liquidity depends on cash on hand, cash provided by operations, working capital, and borrowing power.

The *ratio of cash to current liabilities* directly measures the cash currently available to pay all liabilities due within twelve months, including long-term debt payments due during that period. Then compare cash flow from operating activities to current liabilities to see if operations will generate adequate cash.

The main focus of liquidity analysis is working capital (current assets minus current liabilities). All current assets are theoretically convertible to cash within a year, and thus are available to provide liquidity in a crisis. The current ratio is the most common measure:

Current ratio = Current assets/Current liabilities

In most industries, a ratio of about 1.3 is considered the minimum desired, and 2.0 or more shows healthy liquidity.

The *quick ratio*, however, is a better measure for emergencies. The quick ratio excludes current assets like inventory and prepaid expenses that do not necessarily imply "quick cash":

Quick ratio = (Cash + Accounts receivable)/Current liabilities

When studying working capital, however, be aware that very high working capital may indicate poor utilization of assets. The best managements find ways to operate successfully while minimizing the cash required (and thus also minimizing working capital). *Asset turnover ratios* are measures of the efficiency with which working capital is used:

- Low *accounts receivable turnover* (revenue divided by accounts receivable) may indicate collection problems.
- Low *inventory turnover* (cost of revenue divided by inventory) may indicate inefficient buying, sales or production problems, or increasing inventory obsolescence.
- If included in the statement or notes, the trend of the *classification of inventory* into raw materials, work in progress, and finished goods, is useful. Increases in work in progress and finished goods may indicate a sales shortfall and a forthcoming write-off; raw materials are less risky, because they can often be sold if raising cash becomes necessary.
- *Accounts payable turnover* (purchases divided by accounts payable) is a two-edged sword. Low turnover shows that payments are being stretched, which may mean cash flow problems and lead to vendors shutting off credit—that is, poor liquidity. On the other hand, lower turnover may be positive, indicating that the company has improved its cash management. This is one of a number of examples of the earlier point that financial statement analysis often cannot be used without further knowledge; its function is often more to raise questions than to answer them.

Borrowing power is the last component of liquidity, so to speak. The usual sequence of liquidity analysis is to look first at cash on hand, plus assets readily convertible to cash, versus current liabilities. If this is inadequate, will operations provide the cash to discharge the liabilities? If still inadequate, can available working capital be "stretched" by more effective employment? Finally, if working capital is still inadequate, does the company have the borrowing power to make up the difference?

A company's specific current borrowing power can be determined from information in the notes (and *Management's Discussion of Financial Condition and Operations*, if the company is public) about credit facilities available, and particularly unused balances of credit lines. If these do not exist, judge whether the company has the financial capacity to borrow. Borrowing capacity generally depends on equity, past and prospective profitability, the value of particular types of assets that may be used as collateral, and the amount of financial leverage (debt to capital ratio) that the company is allowed, or is willing to handle. A successful company with little debt and plenty of hard assets can almost surely borrow money if needed, while a marginal company with high debt probably cannot.

In summary, negative equity is an immediate, direct threat to survival. Negative retained earnings, a high ratio of debt to capital, high interest rates, high intangible equity, and poor liquidity represent problems that could be potential survival threats in time.

13

Profit and Loss

The accounting vehicle used to describe the success of a company is the profit and loss (P&L) statement, also called the *operating statement* or the *income statement*. The equation for profit is

$$\text{Profit} = \text{Revenue} - \text{Expense}$$

"Loss" is a negative profit. *Earnings* is used synonymously with profit, and *net income* is the same as net earnings or net profit or *profit after tax*.

Profit differs substantially from cash flow because of the generally accepted accounting principles (GAAP) of conservatism and realization (including as revenue only that which has been earned), and particularly the principle of matching in time any receipts with the costs incurred to generate them.

Revenue is actual or expected gross receipts from products and services, adjusted in time in accordance with GAAP. *Sales* is sometimes used synonymously with revenue, but also sometimes used more narrowly to denote revenue from products, as opposed to service revenue. *Expense* is actual or expected disbursements, adjusted in time in accordance with GAAP. Let's illustrate how timing considerations affect revenue and expense for a computer manufacturer who sells direct to business customers on credit.

Illustrating Revenue and Expense Treatment

Customer orders for this manufacturer's computers are firm commitments to buy them. Should then the revenue for such a computer be credited when the order is received? No, because the revenue has not

125

been earned at this time—something may happen that makes delivery impossible. At the other extreme, should the revenue not be credited until the customer pays for the computer? No, the proper way is to record revenue when the customer accepts the computer. The forthcoming payment is then entered as an *account receivable* until collected. This lets revenue measure success in sales and production, while the size and age of accounts receivable measure success in collection of debts.

The timing considerations that go into the determination of expense are more complicated. Remember that the guiding principle is *matching* revenue with the costs required to generate it.

Consider the factory equipment used in making the computer. This equipment has been there for some time and is expected to continue in use for a few more years. It would be equally misleading either to charge the total equipment cost to this month's revenue, or to consider it free because it was bought some time ago. The proper way is to charge a fair portion of that equipment cost to each computer on which it is used.

How is that fair portion determined? Such equipment is an investment needed and used to produce revenue over a number of years, so it is recorded when bought as *fixed assets*. A useful life is estimated at that time (before it would wear out or have to be replaced by new technology). It would then be *depreciated* over that useful life, and the cost of it *amortized*, or spread, over that same time period. There are various acceptable ways to do this. One common, simple way is straight-line depreciation: if the useful life is five years, one-fifth of the cost is charged to expense in each of those five years, or one-sixtieth each month. The resulting monthly expense, then, effectively charges a portion of the equipment cost to each computer shipped during that month.

Consider the parts and raw materials that go into the computers. These are bought in quantity and, again, it would be unrealistic either to "expense" such a quantity when received or to consider them free on the production floor because they were already on hand. They also have value separately until used in a computer. Therefore, such parts and materials are recorded as *inventory* when purchased and remain there through production until computers are shipped to customers. At that point, inventory is reduced, and the same amount of expense is recorded.

Consider the labor of producing the computers. This is called *direct labor* because it is directly involved in generating revenue. Even such a direct cost may not immediately be recorded in the P&L: work done this month on a computer shipped next month is held in inventory until shipment.

On the other hand, *indirect labor*, like production planning and supervisory costs, contributes costs to production but cannot be realistically assigned to a single product. It is allocated across all products according to a consistent formula. Thus, it also finds its way into the P&L when computers are shipped to customers.

There are numerous other examples, but these are sufficient to show that receipts and disbursements are often unrecognizably different from revenue and expense. As we have shown in many ways, receipts and disbursements themselves do not give a realistic picture of financial health and success. Their timing is determined by other factors, ranging from convenience to payment policies to sophisticated inventory optimization schemes. The complex "matching" P&L reasoning is necessary to measure business success.

Explaining the P&L Statement

The following is the ABC Corp. P&L Statement.

ABC Corp. Profit and Loss Statement

Revenue	$40,000
Cost of revenue	(29,000)
Gross profit	11,000
Operating expense	
Selling, general and administrative expense	(4,000)
Research and development	(3,000)
Profit from operations	4,000
Other income or expense	(1,000)
Profit before tax	3,000
Income tax provision	(1,200)
Net income	$1,800

The P&L statement always starts with revenue and is a series of conventional subtractions from that revenue which culminates in net income (net profit).

GAAP require the distinction between *cost of revenue* and *operating expense*. (Cost of revenue is also called *cost of goods sold* or *cost of sales*.) The former includes all costs associated with the production of revenue, including indirect expense. In a manufacturing business, this generally includes all factory costs—labor, material, and equipment depreciation—plus labor and other costs associated with purchasing, planning, factory management, and the like.

Operating expense, then, is costs involved in operating the business but not directly related to production of revenue. The two items under operating expense in the ABC Corp. P&L statement typify how it is reported. *Selling, general and administrative expense* includes sales costs and such things as company management, accounting, human resources, and legal expenses. *Research and development* refers to costs of bringing on new products.

The distinction between cost of revenue and operating expense varies with the type of business. For example, unlike manufacturing, distribution businesses usually include only material costs of products sold in cost of revenue; all labor and other costs are considered operating expense. The difference between revenue and cost of revenue is called *gross profit*. Gross profit minus operating expense is called *profit from operations*.

Other income or expense, then, presents items like interest or settlements of claims that affect company finances but are not related to its basic business. The difference between profit from operations and other income or expense is called *profit before tax*. Finally, the difference between profit before tax and *net income* is only income tax; that is, all other kinds of tax expense are included in the other expense categories.

These conventional intermediate profits are presented for good reason and are commonly measured by *margins*, which are percentage measures of profitability relative to sales.

- Gross profit shows the success of the company's products and services in a narrow sense.

  Gross margin = Gross profit/Revenue

- Profit from operations shows the success of the company's business, itself, before any extraneous matters or events.

  Operating margin = Profit from operations/Revenue

- Profit before tax indicates the total success of the business before sharing that success with Uncle Sam. Finally, net income shows what the owners actually earned from the company after all revenue and all expense.

$$\text{Profit margin} = \text{Net income/Revenue}$$

Certain events may cause additional line items between profit from operations and net income (not shown on the ABC Corp. P&L statement). *Extraordinary items* are unusual *and* infrequent profits or losses, occurrences unrelated to usual business activities and not expected to occur again. An example is loss from a fire. *Nonrecurring items* are unusual *or* infrequent profits or losses, such as a gain or loss from the sale of a fixed asset. If any business operations have been sold or shut down during the year, *profit from discontinued operations* is presented separately. (If the P&L statement contains this last item, profit from operations becomes *profit from continuing operations*.) If the statement contains any of these, net income is not predictive of future results. In that case, the only profit number that has predictive value is profit from continuing operations.

Analyzing the P&L Statement

Look first at *net income*. You would like it to be positive and adequate relative to sales (expressed as the various *margins*), equity, and capital for the industry and for current conditions. How does it compare with recent years?

The best measures of financial success are *return on equity (ROE)* and *return on capital (ROC)*. The former measures the return on the owners' investment:

$$\text{ROE} = \text{Net income/Equity}$$

That measure obviously interests owners, because they have other places to invest their money and would like a return from the business that is consistent with their risk. However, ROC is a better measure of business success, because it measures the return on the total amount invested in the company:

$$\text{ROC} = \text{Net income/Capital}$$
$$= \text{Net income/(Equity + Long-term liabilities)}$$

In evaluating net income, high quality is important; that is, profit accompanied by cash. A high *ratio of operating cash flow to net income* is an indicator of quality earnings. If earnings have low quality, reasons must be sought in the P&L numbers and in the notes. For example, refinancing debt can generate noncash profit by lowering debt, but it may require increased future negative cash flow and interest expense. That profit is at best of low quality, at worst a mirage. Inventory revaluation produces either noncash profit (if revalued upward) or loss. And so on.

Interest expense (spelled out in the notes if it is only included in other income/expense in the statement) indicates to what extent the company is "working for the banks"; that is, how much of the operating profit has to be paid out as cost of money borrowed. If more than half the profit from operations disappears in interest payments, the company is on shaky ground; a downturn could quickly result in difficulty in meeting financial obligations.

If *backlog* (unfilled firm orders) is included in the P&L statement or elsewhere in the annual report, it is an indicator of future revenue. However, an understanding of the business is necessary to interpret the importance of backlog. To take an extreme example, a business consisting totally of one-year service contracts, all of which renew every January 1, would have backlog that declines continuously across the year. Year-end backlog would be zero for such a business, but that really means nothing relative to its success.

The notes should be studied for *contingencies* that may have large adverse impact on profit in the future. Such adverse contingencies are usually claims or lawsuits of one sort or another.

In summary, negative net income, low-quality earnings, a level of profit that gives inadequate margins and returns, and interest expense that uses up most of profit from operations are all indicators of lack of success and potential survival threats.

14

Summary

Because financial statement analysis is such a broad subject, possibly involving so many sophisticated measures of financial performance, we should end with a summary of the applicability of the subject to office professionals, and their use of such analysis.

1. Office professionals' working concerns with analysis of financial statements are not as investors; rather, their concerns are whether their own companies, competitors, or vendors will survive in a condition that will avoid layoffs, reduced products and services, and restructurings. The conditions for business survival are profitability, positive cash flow, and the ability to meet both long- and short-term financial obligations. The ability to meet short-term obligations is called liquidity, lack of which can shut down even profitable, low-debt companies.

2. To be worth analyzing, financial statements must be audited, meaning independently verified, rather than compiled. Public company statements are always audited, but many private companies only supply compiled statements. Other analysis limitations are that foreign companies have different standards and practices, firm conclusions cannot be drawn just from numbers without underlying knowledge, profit can be managed in the short term, and there are no values or ratios that are ideal for all companies.

3. Within these limitations, financially healthy and successful companies show the following:

   - No qualification of the auditor's letter; that is, no auditor's opinion that a direct threat to survival exists.
   - No survival threats noted in the form 10-K (if the company is public) or in the notes to the financial statements.

- If the company is public, a reassuring and convincing section on liquidity in *Management's Discussion of Financial Conditions and Operations*.
- Positive cash flow, at least over a few years.
- Sufficient cash flow from operations to pay the current dividends, service debt (make both principal and interest payments), and, together with cash flow from financing, to fund needed investments.
- Positive equity (net of intangible assets) and retained earnings.
- A reasonable debt to capital ratio, relative to the industry and current conditions.
- Interest rates on debt within a point or two of the prime rate.
- Good liquidity, evidenced by cash on hand, cash flow from operating activities, working capital and its employment, and borrowing power.
- Positive net income, made up of high-quality earnings (indicated by a high ratio of operating cash flow to net income).
- Enough net income to provide adequate returns on equity and capital.
- Margins of all kinds that compare favorably with the industry and current conditions.

4. The following indicate direct and immediate threats to survival, and important relationships should be avoided with such companies:

   - Negative equity, which means that the company is technically bankrupt.
   - A qualified auditor's letter.

5. The following are indicators of lack of financial health and success that suggest caution in considering important relationships; they may threaten survival over time if not corrected by management:

   - Threatening legal proceedings and/or obligations noted in the form 10-K or notes to the financial statements.
   - Cash flow that is negative, or insufficient to pay current dividends, service debt, or, together with financing, fund needed investments.

- Negative retained earnings.
- High debt to capital ratio, relative to the industry and current conditions.
- High interest rates and/or interest expense that "uses up" most of profit from operations.
- Deficiencies in cash flow, working capital, and borrowing power that indicate poor liquidity.
- Negative net income or profit levels that give low margins and returns relative to the industry and current conditions.

We cannot know the future, but the current financial statements indicate whether a company is moving in a positive direction and if it has the resources to overcome problems that are evident or may occur. The report of independent public accountants, the three statements, and the notes to financial statements show whether

- Current survival threats actually or possibly exist
- Cash flow and profit cover needs and provide a healthy return on investment
- Assets are adequate relative to liabilities, both short- and long-term
- Liquidity is sufficient to survive adverse events

Glossary of Financial Terms

accounts payable Amounts owed by a business for purchases received and accepted.

accounts receivable Money owed to a business by customers for products and services received and accepted.

accrual accounting An accounting basis in which revenue is recorded when earned and costs and balance sheet changes are recorded when commitments are made. Large, one-time expenses can also be averaged over the year or a portion thereof.

accrued expense An anticipated cost recorded as expense before the actual expenditure is made.

accumulated depreciation The total depreciation of a fixed asset from its purchase to the present time.

allocated costs Costs of one type that are assigned or charged to costs of other types. For example, facility costs may be *allocated* to all organizational units using the facility.

amortization Prorating the cost of an asset, liability, or expenditure over a specified period of time.

asset Anything owned that has monetary value.

asset turnover ratio A measure of the efficiency of asset employment, expressed as the ratio of a pertinent parameter, such as revenue, to the asset.

audit In accounting, an independent, professional evaluation of the financial condition of a company.

backlog Orders received but not yet delivered. Also called orders backlog and sales backlog.

balance sheet The financial statement that shows the assets, liabilities, and equity of a business as of a certain date.

bond An interest-bearing certificate that promises to pay the holder a specified sum on a specified date.

book value The same as equity.

budget The financial expression of plans and expected results for a future period, typically a year.

burden rate The percentage rate at which a cost burden is added to particular other costs.

capital The amount invested in a business, equal to equity plus long-term liabilities, or fixed assets plus working capital.

capital expenditure The purchase of equipment and the like that will be accounted for as fixed assets and depreciated over a multiyear period.

capitalized lease An accounting term for a lease that has to be shown as a liability on the balance sheet.

cash Money: checks, bank accounts, or currency. Business usage generally includes cash equivalents.

cash accounting An accounting basis in which revenue, expense, and balance sheet items are recorded when cash is paid or received.

cash equivalents A term of accounting for things that can quickly be converted to cash at known value, such as U.S. Treasury bills.

cash flow The increase or decrease in the cash of a business.

cash flow statement The financial statement that describes cash flow of a business over a particular period of time.

common stock The instrument that gives evidence of the ownership of a corporation.

compilation In accounting, financial statements based on management information without independent evaluation.

contingent liability A liability that may or may not come into existence.

contract An agreement between two or more parties, in which each party binds itself to do or forbear some act, and each acquires a right to what the other promises.

cost burden The increase in a particular cost as the result of allocating another type of cost to it.

cost of revenue The direct costs of producing revenue, burdened by closely associated indirect costs. Often called cost of sales or cost of goods sold.

cost pool A grouping of costs for the purpose of allocation to, or identification with, particular cost centers, products, or services. Common cost pools are various overhead costs, general and administrative costs, and corporate headquarters costs.

current asset Cash and any other asset convertible into cash within a year.

current liability An obligation that must be discharged within a year.

days inventory The amount of inventory relative to the cost of revenue, expressed in "days" typically as 365 times inventory divided by annual cost of revenue.

days payables The amount of accounts payable relative to total material purchased, expressed in "days" typically as 365 times accounts payable divided by annual material purchases.

days receivables The amount of accounts receivable relative to revenue, expressed in "days" typically as 365 times accounts receivable divided by annual revenue.

debt Broadly, any liability. More narrowly and more commonly, money borrowed from, and owed to, another person or institution.

deferred revenue A liability representing advance receipts for products and services to be supplied in the future.

depreciation The gradual decline in value of an asset because of use or age; the expense arising therefrom.

direct expense Cost directly associated with production of specific revenue.

direct labor Labor cost directly associated with production of specific revenue.

disbursement An amount of cash paid out.

dividend Money paid by a corporation to its stockholders, a given amount per share decided by the board of directors.

double-entry bookkeeping The accounting process by which every transaction results in two balancing entries.

earnings The same as profit.

equity The accounting value of a business, equal to assets minus liabilities. Commonly used interchangeably with book value, net asset value, net worth, and stockholders' equity.

expense Past, current, or future cost recorded in a period in accordance with generally accepted accounting principles.

extraordinary items In accounting, items in the profit and loss statement that are both unusual and infrequent.

financial leverage The multiplying effect from debt that owners get on the return on their investment.

finished goods inventory The portion of inventory that consists of goods and products ready for sale.

fiscal year   The twelve-month period for which financial results are prepared and reported. It may be different, by company choice, from the calendar year.

fixed asset   An asset that has long-term value.

fixed expense   An expense that does not vary with revenue over a relevant range of revenue amount.

fringe benefit   Payment by a company for things of value to, and for, the use of employees, such as insurance and vacations.

future value   The value at a given time in the future of an amount of cash presently available, assuming that it can earn a particular interest rate.

general and administrative expense (G&A)   Cost necessary to operate a business but not associated directly with the production of revenue, such as the cost of accounting.

generally accepted accounting principles (GAAP)   The set of rules by and for the accounting profession that govern accounting practice and the preparation of financial statements.

good will   The value of a company's reputation, equal to the difference between market value and book value if and when a company is acquired by another.

gross margin   A percentage measure of profitability, equal to revenue minus cost of revenue divided by revenue.

gross profit   The difference between revenue and cost of revenue.

income statement   The same as profit and loss statement.

indirect expense   Cost that is not directly related or assignable to individual products or services.

intangible assets   Assets, such as patents and good will, whose value is intellectual, rather than physical.

inventory   The physical material and products that a business owns for future production of revenue.

lease   An agreement whereby the lessee acquires the right to property owned by the lessor for a specified period of time.

liability   Something of value owed by a business. A valid claim that someone holds on assets of the business.

line of credit   An agreement by which a given amount of money is made available to a borrower on a recurring basis.

liquidity   The ability to pay current and short-term obligations.

loan   The exchange of money in return for the receiver's obligation to repay.

long-term liability   Any obligation that need not be discharged within one year.

margin   A percentage measure of profitability relative to sales.

market value The amount investors are willing to pay for a company at a given time.

net income Revenue minus all expense for a period, the net financial gain for a business during that period.

net present value (NPV) The algebraic sum of the present values of a future stream of cash flows.

net worth The same as equity.

nonrecurring items In accounting, items in the profit and loss statement that are either unusual or infrequent.

note payable Evidence of a short-term debt owed by a company, whose amount is entered as a current liability on its balance sheet.

note receivable Evidence of a short-term debt owed to a company, whose amount is entered as a current asset on its balance sheet.

operating expense In accounting, expense that is not part of cost of revenue. More generally, the continuing expense needed to operate a business.

operating lease An accounting term for a lease that can be treated as only periodic expense, not a liability.

operating statement The same as the profit and loss statement.

orders received Binding agreements by customers to buy products or services from a company for future delivery.

other income or expense Profit or expense not related to the basic business of a company, such as interest expense.

overhead Indirect cost in a particular function or activity, closely associated with production of revenue but not assignable to individual products or services.

paid-in capital Additional equity investment beyond the par value of company stock.

par value An arbitrary value assigned to a share of stock, usually around $1.

preferred stock A kind of ownership that carries the right to a fixed dividend, but no vote or voice in company affairs.

prepaid expense An asset representing payment for purchases not yet received or used.

present value The value today of an amount of cash available in the future, associated with a particular interest rate.

profit Revenue minus expense, the financial gain of a business.

profit after tax Revenue minus all expense, including federal income tax, the same as net income.

profit before tax Profit before accounting for federal income tax.

profit from continuing operations Profit from operations, net of any effect of operations discontinued during the period.

profit from operations   Profit from the normal activities of a business, equal to gross profit minus operating expense.

profit margin   A percentage measure of profit equal to revenue minus total expense divided by revenue.

purchase order   A document that specifies everything needed to purchase goods and services.

purchase request   The document that specifies purchased items needed by an organization.

quick ratio   A measure of liquidity, equal to cash plus accounts receivable divided by current liabilities.

raw materials inventory   The portion of inventory that consists of purchased material that will be used to make revenue-producing products, and the purchase cost of that material.

receipts   Amounts of cash taken in, or received.

retained earnings   The total amount of income retained over time for use by a business, equal to all past income minus dividends paid out.

return on assets (ROA)   Net income divided by assets, an asset-related measure of return on investment.

return on capital (ROC)   Net income divided by capital, a measure of the percentage of total investment earned by the business.

return on equity (ROE)   Net income divided by equity, a measure of the return on the owners' investment.

return on investment (ROI)   For an entire business, synonymous with return on capital. For a given investment within a business, the ratio of cash flow that will result to the amount of the investment.

return on net assets   The same as return on equity.

revenue   The amount of past, current, and future receipts that are earned and recorded in a given period, in accordance with generally accepted accounting principles.

salary   Fixed amount paid per period to an employee for work.

sales   Generally used interchangeably with revenue, but sometimes restricted to only the revenue that results from the purchase of products by customers, as opposed to service revenue.

secured loan   A loan for which collateral is pledged.

solvency   A company's ability to pay long-term obligations; synonymous with survival.

specification   A statement of the characteristics or requirements of a product, process, or service.

stockholders' equity   Generally the same as equity, although, strictly speaking, it refers only to the equity of a corporation.

tangible asset   An asset whose value is physical.

tangible equity   Equity computed after subtracting out all intangible assets.

term loan   A loan for a specified period of time.

time value of money   Recognition that money available today is more valuable than the same amount available in the future.

turnover   In the U.S., the rate at which a current asset is used and replaced, expressed as the ratio of a year's revenue to the amount of the asset. (In the United Kingdom, turnover is synonymous with revenue.)

unsecured loan   A loan that specifies no collateral and thus relies on the general creditworthiness of the borrower.

variable expense   Expense that varies with revenue.

variance   The amount by which an actual financial parameter, such as a cost, differs from its standard or budgeted value.

wages   Pay to an employee for work by the hour or by the piece.

warranty   A contractual promise that products will perform as specified over a given period of time.

work in progress inventory   The portion of inventory that consists of partially complete products, and the associated burdened labor and material costs.

working capital   Current assets minus current liabilities, a measure of a company's ability to fund short-term operations.

Index